HUGH POULTON is a specialist in Eastern European/ Balkan affairs. He studied at the School of Slavonic and East European Studies at London University and at Skopje University, Macedonia, Yugoslavia. He has travelled extensively in the Balkans and understands several Balkan languages.

THE MINNESOTA LAWYERS INTERNATIONAL HUMAN RIGHTS COMMITTEE (MLIHRC) who wrote the section on Albania, is an independent, non-governmental organization of over 800 lawyers, scholars and judges dedicated to the promotion of human rights worldwide. They have been compiling information on human rights in Albania for several years.

SIZE 2
DR
24
.P6
1989

D1599543

British Library Cataloguing in Publication Data
Poulton, Hugh
Minorities in the Balkans
1.   Balkan countries. Social minorities
I.   Title
II.   Minority Rights Group
III. Series 305'.0946

ISBN No 0 946690 71 5

First published October 1989

Printed by
Expedite Graphic Limited
Murray House, 3 Vandon Street
London SW1H 0AG

Minorities in the Balkans

HUGH POULTON with MLIHRC

The report that follows has been commissioned, and is published, by the Minority Rights Group as a contribution to public understanding of the problem which forms its subject. It does not necessarily represent, in every detail and in all its aspects, the collective view of the Group.

To receive the reports of the Minority Rights Group on a regular basis please take out a subscription. 5 reports annually for £12.00/US$25.

For details of the other reports published by the Minority Rights Group, please see the inside back cover.

The cover photo shows Turkish refugees at Edirne on the Turkish-Bulgarian Border 1989 (Roger Hutchings, *The Observer*, London)

THE UNITED NATIONS
UNIVERSAL DECLARATION OF HUMAN RIGHTS

Whereas recognition of the inherent dignity and of the equal and inalienable rights of all members of the human family is the foundation of freedom, justice and peace in the world.

Whereas disregard and contempt for human rights have resulted in barbarous acts which have outraged the conscience of mankind, and the advent of a world in which human beings shall enjoy freedom of speech and belief and freedom from any fear and want has been proclaimed as the highest aspiration of the common people,

Whereas it is essential, if a man is not to be compelled to have recourse, as a last resort, to rebellion against tyranny and oppression, that human rights should be protected by the rule of law,

Whereas it is essential to promote the development of friendly relations between nations,

Whereas the peoples of the United Nations have in the Charter reaffirmed their faith in fundamental human rights, in the dignity and worth of the human person and in the equal rights of men and women and have determined to promote social progress and better standards of life in larger freedom,

Whereas Member States have pledged themselves to achieve, in co-operation with the United Nations, the promotion of universal respect for and observance of human rights and fundamental freedoms,

Whereas a common understanding of these rights and freedoms is of the greatest importance for the full realization of this pledge,

Now, Therefore,

THE GENERAL ASSEMBLY
proclaims

THIS UNIVERSAL DECLARATION OF HUMAN RIGHTS as a common standard of achievement for all peoples and all nations, to the end that every individual and every organ of society, keeping this Declaration constantly in mind, shall strive by teaching and education to promote respect for these rights and freedoms and by progressive measures, national and international, to secure their universal and effective recognition and observance, both among the peoples of Member States themselves and among the peoples of territories under their jurisdiction.

Article 1. All human beings are born free and equal in dignity and rights. They are endowed with reason and conscience and should act towards one another in a spirit of brotherhood.

Article 2. Everyone is entitled to all the rights and freedoms set forth in this Declaration, without distinction of any kind, such as race, colour, sex, language, religion, political or other opinion, national or social origin, property, birth or other status.

Furthermore, no distinction shall be made on the basis of the political, jurisdictional or international status of the country or territory to which a person belongs, whether it be independent, trust, non-self-governing or under any other limitation of sovereignty.

Article 3. Everyone has the right to life, liberty and security of person.

Article 4. No one shall be held in slavery or servitude; slavery and the slave trade shall be prohibited in all their forms.

Article 5. No one shall be subjected to torture or to cruel, inhuman or degrading treatment or punishment.

Article 6. Everyone has the right to recognition everywhere as a person before the law.

Article 7. All are equal before the law and are entitled without any discrimination to equal protection of the law. All are entitled to equal protection against any discrimination in violation of this Declaration and against any incitement to such discrimination.

Article 8. Everyone has the right to an effective remedy by the competent national tribunals for acts violating the fundamental rights granted him by the constitution or by law.

Article 9. No one shall be subjected to arbitrary arrest, detention or exile.

Article 10. Everyone is entitled in full equality to a fair and public hearing by an independent and impartial tribunal, in the determination of his rights and obligations and of any criminal charge against him.

Article 11. (1) Everyone charged with a penal offence has the right to be presumed innocent until proved guilty according to law in a public trial at which he has had all the guarantees necessary for his defence.

(2) No one shall be held guilty of any penal offence on account of any act or omission which did not constitute a penal offence, under national or international law, at the time when it was committed. Nor shall a heavier penalty be imposed than the one that was applicable at the time the penal offence was committed.

Article 12. No one shall be subjected to arbitrary interference with his privacy, family, home or correspondence, nor to attacks upon his honour and reputation. Everyone has the right to the protection of the law against such interference or attacks.

Article 13. (1) Everyone has the right to freedom of movement and residence within the borders of each state.

(2) Everyone has the right to leave any country, including his own, and to return to his country.

Article 14. (1) Everyone has the right to seek and to enjoy in other countries asylum from persecution.

(2) This right may not be invoked in the case of prosecutions genuinely arising from non-political crimes or from acts contrary to the purposes and principles of the United Nations.

Article 15. (1) Everyone has the right to a nationality.

(2) No one shall be arbitrarily deprived of his nationality nor denied the right to change his nationality.

Article 16. (1) Men and women of full age, without any limitation due to race, nationality or religion, have the right to marry and to found a family. They are entitled to equal rights as to marriage, during marriage and at its dissolution.

(2) Marriage shall be entered into only with the free and full consent of the intending spouses.

(3) The family is the natural and fundamental group unit of society and is entitled to protection by society and the State.

Article 17. (1) Everyone has the right to own property alone as well as in association with others.

(2) No one shall be arbitrarily deprived of his property.

Article 18. Everyone has the right to freedom of thought, conscience and religion; this right includes freedom to change his religion or belief, and freedom, either alone or in community with others and in public or private, to manifest his religion or belief in teaching, practice, worship and observance.

Article 19. Everyone has the right to freedom of opinion and expression; this right includes freedom to hold opinions without interference and to seek, receive and impart information and ideas through any media and regardless of frontiers.

Article 20. (1) Everyone has the right to freedom of peaceful assembly and association.

(2) No one may be compelled to belong to an association.

Article 21. (1) Everyone has the right to take part in the government of his country, directly or through freely chosen representatives.

(2) Everyone has the right of equal access to public service in his country.

(3) The will of the people shall be the basis of the authority of government; this will shall be expressed in periodic and genuine elections which shall be by universal and equal suffrage and shall be held by secret vote or by equivalent free voting procedures.

Article 22. Everyone, as a member of society, has the right to social security and is entitled to realization, through national effort and international co-operation and in accordance with the organization and resources of each State, of the economic, social and cultural rights indispensable for his dignity and the free development of his personality.

Article 23. (1) Everyone has the right to work, to free choice of employment, to just and favourable conditions of work and to protection against unemployment.

(2) Everyone, without any discrimination, has the right to equal pay for equal work.

(3) Everyone who works has the right to just and favourable remuneration ensuring for himself and his family an existence worthy of human dignity, and supplemented, if necessary, by other means of social protection.

(4) Everyone has the right to form and to join trade unions for the protection of his interest.

Article 24. Everyone has the right to rest and leisure, including reasonable limitation of working hours and periodic holidays with pay.

Article 25. (1) Everyone has the right to a standard of living adequate for the health and well-being of himself and of his family, including food, clothing, housing and medical care and necessary social services, and the right to security in the event of unemployment, sickness, disability, widowhood, old age or other lack of livelihood in circumstances beyond his control.

(2) Motherhood and childhood are entitled to special care and assistance. All children, whether born in or out of wedlock, shall enjoy the same social protection.

Article 26. (1) Everyone has the right to education. Education shall be free, at least in the elementary and fundamental stages. Elementary education shall be compulsory. Technical and professional education shall be made generally available and higher education shall be equally accessible to all on the basis of merit.

(2) Education shall be directed to the full development of the human personality and to the strengthening of respect for human rights and fundamental freedoms. It shall promote understanding, tolerance and friendship among all nations, racial or religious groups, and shall further the activities of the United Nations for the maintenance of peace.

(3) Parents have a prior right to choose the kind of education that shall be given to their children.

Article 27. (1) Everyone has the right freely to participate in the cultural life of the community, to enjoy the arts and to share in scientific advancement and its benefits.

(2) Everyone has the right to the protection of the moral and material interests resulting from any scientific, literary or artistic production of which he is the author.

Article 28. Everyone is entitled to a social and international order in which the rights and freedoms set forth in this Declaration can be fully realized.

Article 29. (1) Everyone has duties to the community in which alone the free and full development of his personality is possible.

(2) In the exercise of his rights and freedoms, everyone shall be subject only to such limitations as are determined by law solely for the purpose of securing due recognition and respect for the rights and freedoms of others and of meeting the just requirements of morality, public order and the general welfare in a democratic society.

(3) These rights and freedoms may in no case be exercised contrary to the purposes and principles of the United Nations.

Article 30. Nothing in this Declaration may be interpreted as implying for any State, group or person any right to engage in any activity or to perform any act aimed at the destruction of any of the rights and freedoms set forth herein.

PREFACE

From May 1989 the world press was alerted to the repression of ethnic Turks in Bulgaria and the subsequent flight of tens of thousands of refugees from Bulgaria into Turkey. Their peaceful protests against forced assimilation had been brutally repressed and between May and September 1989 over 300,000 Bulgarian citizens sought sanctuary in Turkey. They brought with them few possessions and had little hope of a more prosperous future; nevertheless they were determined to end the indignity, humiliation and repression that they suffered in Bulgaria.

The Minority Rights Group has been following events closely in Bulgaria since 1985 and early in 1989 MRG decided to publish a report on minorities in the Balkans, where wars have changed boundaries many times in the last hundred years and where Communism, Christianity and Islam all have a strong influence. It was clear that the state of flux and changes in political attitudes both in the USSR and between the major political and military alliances might lead to radical changes in the old order and in the structures of society, all of which may have profound implications for minorities. The tensions between Greece and Turkey has left the Turkish Community of Western Thrace in Northern Greece particularly exposed while Albania's neglect of human rights and its determined isolationism has led to grave concerns over the treatment of Greek Orthodox Christians in a Communist state. It was clear that if the rights of minorities were to be advanced in practice and constructive ways forward were to be found, some authoritative research was essential in this complex area.

Consequently the Minority Rights Group was delighted to invite Hugh Poulton, a major authority on human rights in the Balkans, to write this report on the plight of minorities in Bulgaria, Macedonia and Greece, and in order to complete this complex mosaic, the Minority Rights Group also invited the Minnesota Lawyers International Human Rights Committee to contribute a section on Albania.

The authors' aim is to provide an authoritative and objective account of minorities in the Balkans, in the light of the common history of Ottoman domination, the emergence of separate Balkan states and the diverse minority peoples contained in these states. It seeks to stimulate a better understanding of the present conflicts, to promote 'minority rights' and to encourage peaceful and just solutions.

The situation in Bulgaria is the most critical because of the Bulgarian authorities' current policy of forcible assimilation of its large minority populations and the ensuing levels of violence this policy has caused. Although it is beyond the scope of this report to cover the enormous subject of the nationality question in Yugoslavia, the situation in the Socialist Republic of Macedonia — one of the Socialist Federal Republics of Yugoslavia's six constituent republics — is covered due to its historical and polemical relationship with both Bulgaria and Greece over the Macedonian issue and its own sizeable minorities. The situation of minorities in Greece, especially in Aegean Macedonia and Western Thrace is included for similar reasons and the whole area along with Albania has historically constituted an entity with many shared cultural aspects. The situation concerning Romania is covered in MRG Report No 37 *Hungarians of Romania*.

Five hundred years of Ottoman Turkish administration, conversion and settlement has resulted in new minority groups such as the Turks and the Pomaks, in addition to already existing minority groups. The rise of modern nationalism in the 19th and early 20th century resulted in the formation of the present states of Greece, Bulgaria, Albania and Yugoslavia. Yet in the first two of these states, nationalism has taken the form of creating, or attempting to create a 'national consciousness' which has largely aimed at the assimilation, absorption or even denial of the existence of minorities.

In **Bulgaria** both the Macedonian and the Pomak minority are considered to be Bulgarians as are the largest Islamic minority, the ethnic Turks, who are the victims of an official campaign to force them to abandon their minority characteristics such as their names, language and religious practices.

In the Yugoslav Republic of **Macedonia** there has been growing friction between the Slav Macedonian majority and the large Albanian minority which has received little publicity in contrast to the situation of the Albanians in the neighbouring provice of Kosovo. In **Greece**, Macedonians have been assimilated into the Greek majority over a number of years while ethnic Turks in Western Thrace claim that they face official discrimination.

Although information is scarce on the situation of the Greek minority in **Albania**, it seems they face assimilatory pressures in addition to the general religious repression faced by Muslims and Christians alike.

The Helsinki monitoring process of human rights in Eastern Europe includes the rights of minority groups. MRG sees this present report on the urgent and explosive situation as an important contribution to the understanding of the situation and as an active instrument for those who want constructive change and human rights for all minorities.

Alan Phillips
Executive Director
MRG
October 1989

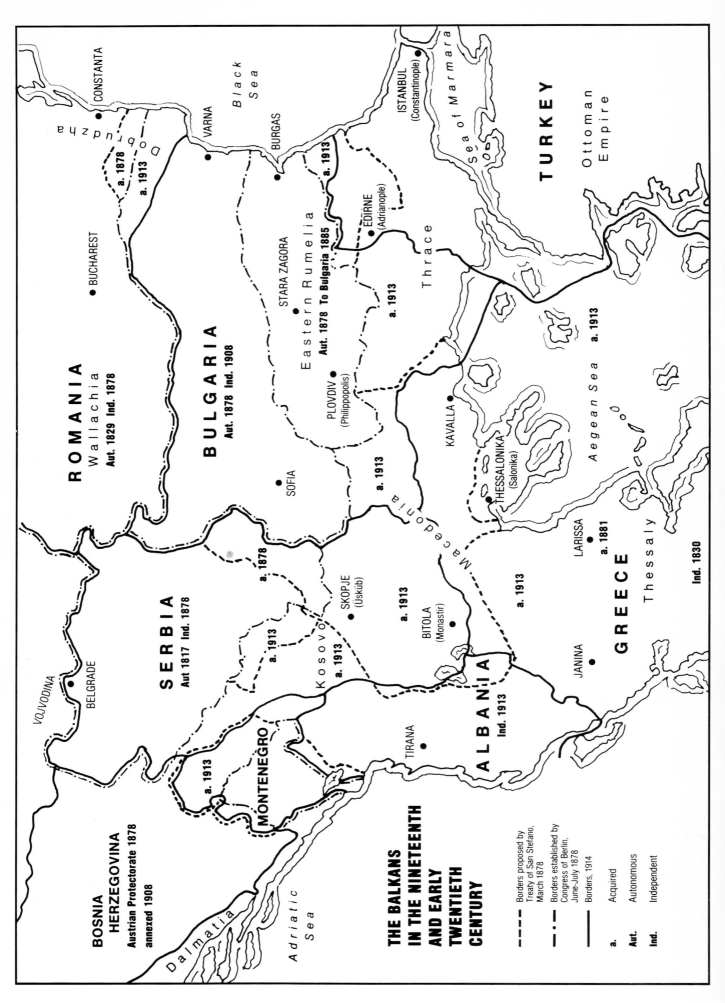

CONSTANTA

Black Sea

ISTANBUL (Constantinople)

Sea of Marmara

TURKEY

Ottoman Empire

Dobrudzha

a. 1878
a. 1913

VARNA

BURGAS

a. 1913

EDIRNE (Adrianople)

Thrace

a. 1913

BUCHAREST

STARA ZAGORA

Eastern Rumelia Aut. 1878 To Bulgaria 1885

a. 1913

ROMANIA

Wallachia Aut. 1829 Ind. 1878

BULGARIA

Aut. 1878 Ind. 1908

PLOVDIV (Philippopolis)

KAVALLA

a. 1913

Aegean Sea

SOFIA

a. 1913

THESSALONIKA (Salonika)

LARISSA

a. 1881

VOJVODINA

BELGRADE

a. 1878

Macedonia

SKOPJE (Üsküb)

a. 1913

BITOLA (Monastir)

JANINA

GREECE

Thessaly

Ind. 1830

SERBIA

Aut 1817 Ind. 1878

a. 1913

a. 1913

Kosovo

a. 1913

a. 1913

MONTENEGRO

a. 1913

TIRANA

ALBANIA

Ind. 1913

Adriatic Sea

Dalmatia

BOSNIA HERZEGOVINA

Austrian Protectorate 1878

annexed 1908

THE BALKANS IN THE NINETEENTH AND EARLY TWENTIETH CENTURY

- - - - Borders proposed by Treaty of San Stefano, March 1878

—·—· Borders established by Congress of Berlin, June–July 1878

——— Borders, 1914

a.   Acquired

Aut.   Autonomous

Ind.   Independent

INTRODUCTION: The peoples of the Balkans; the legacy of the Ottomans; and the rise of local nationalism

The Balkan peninsula in south-east Europe is one of the most ethnically, linguistically and religiously complex areas of the world. Its geographic position has historically resulted in it being disrupted by invaders moving from Asia Minor to Europe or vice-versa. The three oldest peoples in the area under study are the Greeks, the Vlachs (descended from the original Thracians), and the Albanians who claim descent from the ancient Illyrians.

The Slavs, an Indo-European people originating in East-Central Europe had begun to cross the Danube into the Balkans by the 6th century A.D. In the 7th century combined assaults by Slavs and Proto-Bulgarians, a Turkic people from the area between the Urals and the Volga who had come via the steppes north of the Caspian Sea, led to the founding of the first Bulgarian state in 681. In 864 under the direction of their leader Boris, the Proto-Bulgarians converted en masse to Christianity and this greatly helped them to coalesce with the Slavs, who had already been converted, and by the end of the 9th century they were as one people speaking a Slav-based language (Yugoslav historians claim that the Macedonian Slavs have always been a separate people from those in Bulgaria (see pages 23-24).

From the 10th century onwards Gypsies, originating from Northern India, began to arrive into the area. By the end of the 13th century the Serbs, another Slavic people, were establishing hegemony over much of the Balkans and in 1282 King Milutin took Skopje from the Byzantium empire and opened the way for Serbian penetration into Macedonia. Disunity in the Balkans allowed the Ottoman Turks, an Asiatic people who had gradually eroded away the ailing Byzantine empire, to invade the peninsula from Asia Minor in the 14th century through Macedonia and the Maritsa valley. The gradual Ottoman conquest culminated in the defeat of the Serbs at Kosovo Polje in 1389 and opened the way for complete Ottoman conquest of the Balkans and the fall of Constantinople in 1453 saw the end of the Byzantine empire. Large numbers of Serbs moved northwards from Kosovo to escape Ottoman domination and settled on the borders of the Kingdom of Hungary in present-day Vojvodina.

Ottoman rule was to last for almost five centuries over much of the Balkan peninsula. However despite at one time advancing almost to Vienna and looking to threaten Western Europe the Ottoman empire began to decline and by the early 19th century the empire was in a state of decay with its economy stagnant, the once efficient bureaucracy corrupt, and the army demoralized. Simultaneously and to an extent because of this degeneration there appeared the awakening of the Balkan peoples aided by the intervention and interest of the Great Powers especially Russia and Austria-Hungary.

Geographically the Balkan peninsula is very mountainous and communications are difficult and this has resulted in communities tending to be compartmentalized as opposed to unified. Although there were inevitably some people who accepted the religion of the new rulers — the Pomaks of the Rhodope mountains, and the Bosnians in central Yugoslavia — the Ottoman rulers were non-assimilative and multi-national without the technological and institutional facilities for integrating and unifying the subject peoples — unlike in Western Europe where the new 'nation states' were able, for the most part, to transcend regional loyalties. As a result the peoples of the Balkans managed to retain their separate identities and cultures as well as, for many of them, retaining a sense of a former glorious history when they controlled a particular area, which with the national awakenings in the 19th century they once more claimed — often at the expense of their neighbours who likewise made historical claims to the territory in question. Thus the national awakenings which saw the beginnings of the crumbling of Ottoman power in the Balkans by the mid-19th century with the establishment of the Serbian state, in the north around Belgrade, and the Greek state, in the south around Athens, often gave rise to hostility between the previous Ottoman subject people — a hostility that was to reach its zenith in the struggle for Macedonia at the beginning of this century.

The Ottoman empire was until the last quarter of the 19th and first part of the 20th century a theocratic empire whose population was divided not along linguistic lines but by religious affiliation — the *millet* system — and religion has traditionally been one of the main factors in differentiating between various groups. The concept of nationality as expounded in the ideology of nationalism was a late arrival to the Balkans as well as to Turkey.

In the case of the Bulgarians, after the Ottoman invasion, the separate Bulgarian church and the attendant education system were placed under the control of the Greek Orthodox Church and the Greek Patriarch in Istanbul. Thus until the Bulgarian national revival in the 19th century it can be argued that the Bulgarians faced as big a threat of assimilation from the Greeks who controlled the religious services and education both of which were held in Greek, as from the Ottoman Turks. This is illustrated in an old Bulgarian proverb 'Save us Lord from the Bulgarian who becomes a Greek and from the Gypsy who becomes a Turk'. Indeed a crucial factor in the growth of Bulgarian national consciousness was the establishment of the national church, the Exarchate, in 1870 by the Ottoman authorities following a long movement which began in 1820. In 1867 Patriarch Gregory VI had offered an autonomous Bulgarian church but one not to be extended to the parishes in Macedonia. The Bulgarians had refused and called for the populations of the relevant dioceses to decide. The decree of 1870 gave the Exarchate in only 17 dioceses but allowed parishes by two-thirds majority vote of all adult males to choose whether to join and have church services in the vernacular or continue in Greek. This struggle for a national church was a political rather than a religious struggle. The parishes which opted for the vernacular comprised the so-called Greater Bulgaria which was to come into existence following the treaty of San Stefano in 1878 at the end of the Russo-Turkish war of 1875-8. However the Great Powers, notably Britain and Austro-Hungary both of whom feared that such a large Bulgaria dominating the Balkans and straddling the Bosphorus would be a client state of Russia, forced its abandonment and its replacement instead by a severely truncated state at the Treaty of Berlin.

The loss of what most Bulgarians then, and still today, consider to be their natural territory is an important factor in the Bulgarian national psyche and the anniversary of the San Stefano treaty is still celebrated in Bulgaria with greater official pomp than the anniversary of the Treaty of Berlin which followed. Although Bulgaria did succeed in regaining Eastern Rumelia in 1885 much of the 'lost territories' remain outside her borders and are now in present-day Yugoslavia and Greece.

Bulgaria

Bulgaria in outline

The People's Republic of Bulgaria has an area of 110,912 sq.kms. and lies in southeast Europe. It shares borders with four countries: Greece, Romania, Turkey and Yugoslavia and is bounded to the east by the Black Sea.

The modern Bulgarian state was formed from territories of the Ottoman empire in 1878 during the Russo-Turkish war of 1875-78 and mostly comprised the northern half of present-day Bulgaria north of the Stara Planina (the Balkan Mountains). The southern part, formerly called Eastern Rumelia, was added in 1885 and the country declared itself fully independent in 1908.

During World War II, Bulgaria was an ally of Nazi Germany but without ever declaring war against the Soviet Union. However, in September 1944 the Soviet Union declared war on Bulgaria and on 9 September 1944 the Fatherland Front, a coalition of opposition political parties including the Bulgarian Communist Party (BCP), took power. In September 1946 Bulgaria was proclaimed a People's Republic and by 1948 the BCP completely controlled the country.

Bulgaria had a population of 8,917,200 at the end of 1984, of whom 66.2% lived in towns and 33.8% in rural settlements. The capital is Sofia which had 1,182,868 inhabitants in 1984.[1] There are a number of minorities living in Bulgaria of which the most numerous are the ethnic Turks, estimated to number at least 900,000 and maybe as many as one and a half million, and the Gypsies, estimated to number 450,000.

Before World War II Bulgaria was primarily an agricultural producer with a few important mineral resources, mainly lignite and some iron ore. However, since the war there has been rapid industrialization. Two-thirds of Bulgaria's exports now derive from engineering and the steel and petro-chemical industries have been developed. The main crops are wheat, maize, tobacco (Bulgaria is the largest European producer), fruit and vegetables. Agriculture was completely collectivized by 1958; however, the collective farmer is entitled to a private plot of between 20% and 50% of an acre per household. In 1980, 33.5% of the economically active population worked in agriculture.

Bulgaria is a centralized state. The BCP and the communist controlled Agrarian Union are the only permitted political parties. The BCP has been led by Todor Zhivkov since 1954; he is also Chairman of the State Council — the titular head of state. The supreme legislative body is the National Assembly, composed of 400 deputies elected for a five-year term on the basis of a single list of candidates. The assembly meets three times a year and between sessions it delegates authority to the State Council (elected from among its own members) which is in permanent session. The National Assembly elects the Council of Ministers, the supreme executive authority whose chairman is the Prime Minister. At the local level Bulgaria was until January 1988 divided into 28 districts, each administered by a People's Council, which is elected for a term of two and a half years. However State Council Decree No.2704 abolished the 28 districts (okrags) and replaced them with 8 regions (oblasts) again administered by a People's Council. Bulgaria joined the United Nations in 1955, and is a founder member of the Council for Mutual Economic Assistance, and the Warsaw Pact.

MINORITIES IN BULGARIA

International boundaries
District boundaries (in 1988 the 28 districts were replaced by 8 regions)
Mountainous areas
Areas where ethnic minorities live

Minorities in Bulgaria

The Macedonians

'The Macedonian Question' has historically been one of the most contentious as well as one of the most complicated issues in the Balkans. The Macedonians (a slavic people, not to be confused with the subjects of Phillip of Macedon in antiquity) live in the southwestern regions of the country. Successive censuses have given conflicting figures for the numbers of Macedonians in Bulgaria.

The results of the 1946 Bulgarian census concerning the Macedonian population were never made public by the Bulgarian authorities. However, Yugoslav sources claim that 252,908 people declared themselves as Macedonians in that census.[2] The census of 1956 recorded 187,789 Macedonians, over 95% of whom lived in the Pirin region where they made up 63.8% of the population. However, in the 1965 census the number of people declaring themselves as Macedonian had dropped to only 8750 and in the district of Blagoevgrad which previously had the highest percentage of Macedonians it was less than 1%.[3]

Bulgaria has traditionally claimed that the Macedonians (including those living in Yugoslavia and Greece) are ethnic Bulgarians. However immediately after World War II when Georgi Dimitrov, both of whose parents were from Macedonia, was leader the BCP fully recognized a separate Macedonian nationality and allowed extensive contact between Pirin Macedonia and the newly formed Macedonian Republic in post-war Yugoslavia. Following his death and the break between Yugoslavia and the Soviet Union, Bulgarian unease at this recognition became more apparent and the Bulgarians only admitted that the process of nationality for the Macedonians began in 1918. Later the date was changed to 1944 and at the April plenum of the BCP in 1956 when Todor Zhivkov cemented his power it appears that it was decided no longer to recognize a separate Macedonian nationality.[4] Throughout the early 1960s the Bulgarian authorities, when renewing the compulsory personal identity cards, allegedly issued cards stating that the holder was Bulgarian by ethnicity to those who had previously held cards stating that they were Macedonian.

From the early 1960s there have also reportedly been a number of political trials of people accused of activity based on Macedonian nationalism. For example, a group of inhabitants of Blagoevgrad were tried in 1962 by the District Court of Blagoevgrad on charges of creating a group whose aims were the secession of Pirin Macedonia from the People's Republic of Bulgaria and in 1964 four people from Blagoevgrad were reportedly tried for writing 'We are Macedonians' and 'Long live the Macedonian nation' on a restaurant wall. Since the introduction of the latest Criminal Code in 1968, most of those accused of propagating such 'anti-democratic and nationalist ideology' have been charged under Articles 108 and 109 which deal respectively with 'anti-state agitation and propaganda' and with forming or leading and membership of an illegal group. Article 39 (1) of the People's Militia Law of 1976 (amended on 12 August 1983) also allows administrative punishment (that is without trial), which has reportedly been used to forcibly resettle members of the Macedonian ethnic minority in other areas of the country.[5] According to Yugoslav sources, whole families were forced to move from the Pirin region to other regions in the north because of their affirmation of a Macedonian ethnicity distinct from Bulgarian.[6] At the same time as this repression, the Bulgarian authorities have concentrated resources into the Pirin region, the health resort of Sandanski being a notable example, apparently so as to lessen any possible attraction from neighbouring Yugoslavia.[7]

The Bulgarian Mohammedans (Pomaks)

The Bulgarian Mohammedans, usually called by the originally derogatory term 'Pomaks', are a religious minority. They are Slav Bulgarians who speak Bulgarian as their mother tongue but whose religion and customs are Islamic. They are estimated to number in excess of 150,000 and live in compact settlements in the mountainous regions of the Rhodope mountains in south-western and southern Bulgaria.

Since 1948 the Bulgarian authorities have made repeated attempts to induce the Pomaks to change their names, renounce their faith and become integrated into the socialist Bulgarian state. In the period 1971 to 1973 the authorities pursued a concerted campaign to force the Pomaks to change their names by obliging them to choose new ones from a list of 'official' Bulgarian names.[8] For example a Pomak whose name previously was Mustapha Aliev could choose his new name to be Emil, but his surname would depend traditionally on that of his father so that his new surname depended on what his father chose. However in practice it was often the sons who would choose the new names — the name Emil Dimitrov, a popular Bulgarian singer, was a frequent choice — so that the father would have to change his name accordingly thus reversing the traditional manner by which people are named.

An eyewitness account relating to a town in the southern Rhodope mountains in this period states that in the town square, in front of the House of Culture, a long red table was set out with all the local state and Communist Party officials in attendance. Armed detachments with loaded weapons at the ready were also there to ensure order. The Pomaks were obliged to approach the table one by one over a long red carpet and hand in their old identity papers and receive new ones made out in new Bulgarian names and thank the officials publicly. Some Pomaks, mostly old people but some young ones as well, refused but from that day onwards the old identity papers were invalid for all inhabitants of the town and the official bureaucracy which pervades all aspects of life in Bulgaria refused to recognize them, so that for example no pensions, state salary or money from a bank account could be drawn unless the new cards were used.

There were a number of instances of violent resistance. For example, in 1971 there were riots in Pazardzhik in which two Communist Party functionaries were reportedly killed. The authorities reacted by arresting large numbers of people. Two Pomaks were condemned to death and two others sentenced to 15 years' imprisonment. A group of Pomaks travelled to Sofia and protested against these measures but were stopped near the town of Samakov by the militia and in a violent clash two Pomaks were shot dead and 50 wounded. There were also reported violent clashes in Barutin and around Devin.[9]

According to an eyewitness now living in Turkey, in July 1971 in the village of Ribnovo in Blagoevgrad district two Pomaks — Salih Mehemdov Hatibov and Nevzem Mustafova Issaeva — were publicly hanged in the village for resisting the name-changing and another, Yakub Halilov Mihrin, died in hospital as a result of injuries sustained during a beating by the security forces. From Ribnono alone in the early 1970s, 32 people were imprisoned in Belene prison camp for refusing their new names. According to Huseyin Memisoglu, a former History professor at Sofia University who fled Bulgaria in March 1988, intensive military operations were carried out in May 1972 in Blagoevgrad and surrounding districts against the Pomaks which resulted in the deaths of hundreds of Pomaks who resisted the forced assimilation.[10]

In March 1973 security forces supported by border guards again entered several villages in Blagoevgrad district and went from house to house with prepared lists of Bulgarian names from which the Pomak inhabitants were obliged to select new names. In the violent resistance which ensued at least eight people were reported to have died, including one army officer, and a number of people wounded. Large numbers of Pomaks were arrested, 20 from the village of Kornitsa alone, and sentenced to three to 15 years' imprisonment. About 100 Pomaks were also deported to other areas in Bulgaria.

In this operation, the village of Kornitsa was surrounded by mounted armed police who attacked the villagers assembled in protest against the compulsory name-changing in the village square and allegedly killed seven men. The others fled to their houses and the police went from house to house. One Pomak, Bairam Redzhepov Gaitov, was beaten by the police in his home, arrested and taken to Sofia investigation prison. He was subsequently sentenced to 12 years' imprisonment for 'membership of a group formed to commit offences against the State' and 'dissemination of false information with the aim of undermining the State'. It is reported that he spent the first two years in solitary confinement and that he was beaten and ill-treated in prison in order to extract a confession from him.

His wife and two daughters were deported to a village in the province of Vidin, where his wife and eldest daughter were compelled to do forced labour. His 16-year-old son was sent to a school to learn to be a tractor driver, and reportedly there he was pressured to denounce his father and change his name. When he refused and ran away from the school, he was beaten so savagely that he was subsequently exempt from military service, declared infirm and sent to a mental hospital. He has never fully recovered. Bairam Gaitov was eventually released from prison in 1980.[11]

In prison the Pomaks suffered particularly harsh treatment. If they failed to use or respond to the Bulgarian name assigned to them by the authorities they risked being deprived of their right to visits from their families. In 1975 Amnesty International was informed that about 500 Pomaks were serving prison sentences in Belene prison camp and in 1977 reported that there were 40 to 50 Pomaks held in Stara Zagora Prison, many kept in solitary confinement with reduced rations for periods longer than the maximum 14 days allowed by Bulgarian penal law. Former prisoners from Sara Zagora Prison have alleged that Pomaks have been put for as long as three days in a special concrete cell, 'one metre square', which has a curved floor often covered with water. In winter the water freezes, and prisoners have suffered from kidney diseases and pneumonia.[12]

Demonstrations by Pomaks reportedly began on 15 August 1989 in protest at the authorities apparent refusal to issue passports to people living in the predominantly Pomak area around Gotse Delchev — a new passport law had allowed over 300,000 ethnic Turks to emigrate in the summer of 1989 (see pages 21-22). Protests were reportedly staged in over a dozen villages including Hvostyane, Kornitsa, Lazhnitsa, Breznitsa, Dabnitsa and Blatska. Security forces sealed off at least six villages with unconfirmed reports of killings having occurred during the suppression of these demonstrations.

The Gypsies, Albanians, Tatars, Vlachs and Saraktsani

There is very little information available on the **Gypsy minority** in Bulgaria estimated to number some 450,000 or so with some 45,000 in Sliven alone. While Bulgaria has made a determined effort to raise the living standards and

educational opportunities of the Gypsy minority, the authorities have been equally firm in denying them the right to preserve their own identity and culture through formation of socio-political organizations with only a few local music ensembles allowed. In the period of 1953/4 there was an operation to settle the nomadic Gypsy population, often in the northern plain below the Danube and, in the case of Muslim Gypsies — the majority — to change their names. A similar name-changing campaign to that concerning the Pomaks was reported to have taken place in the late 1970s but few details are available. The restrictions on the practice of Islam which accompanied the crackdown against the Turkish minority in 1984/5 also adversely affected Muslim Gypsies. Despite the assimilation policy, the large settled Gypsy communities in Sliven, and the quarters in Sofia, Varna and Plovdiv remain strongholds of Gypsy social life and the assimilation policies appear to have had little impact. Small scale discrimination against Gypsies continues in everyday life.

Ethnic **Albanians**, estimated to number some 5000 or so and resident in Bulgaria since Albania's break with the USSR in the 1960s, also had their names changed at the same time as the small number of **Muslim Tatars** but again little information is available.[13]

Similarly, little information is available on the **Vlachs**, also known in Bulgaria as the **Karakachani**. The Vlachs are a predominately pastoral people living south of the Danube, primarily in Greece but also in Albania, Yugoslavia and Bulgaria, who speak a form of Romanian. A motion for a resolution to the European Parliament in November 1985 quotes 'recent specialists studies' as indicating that some 400,000 Vlachs live in compact areas in Northern Bulgaria[14] but this figure appears to be widely exaggerated. Vlachs tend to live in scattered communities in mountainous regions like the central Stara Planina range and the Struma valley although many live in the Dobrudzha region, where many Vlach emigres from Macedonia were settled by the Romanian government which controlled the area from the Second Balkan War until 1940, and the coastal areas around Varna. Whatever the figure the Vlachs have been subjected to the same 'Bulgarization' process as the other minorities, excepting the Jews and Armenians, although the process antedates many later assimilation campaigns and there are reports of pressure on Vlachs in the early 1970s. It appears that the language will shortly die out. There is similarly little information on the small number of Greek-speaking **Sarakatsani** who are also transhumant shepherds, who share many customs and traits with the Vlachs, and still survive in the upland pastures.

The assimilation of the ethnic Turks

Background factors

Ethnic Turks began to settle in Bulgaria towards the end of the 14th century and have lived there ever since. They live mostly in compact communities in the south of the country in the Arda river basin and in the northeast in the Dobrudzha region. They also live in scattered communities in the central and eastern Stara Planina (the Balkan Mountains) and in the Rhodope mountains.

Until the most recent campaign to assimilate them, the ethnic Turks were officially recognized as a 'national minority' along with certain other minorities including the Gypsies but excluding the Macedonians and the Pomaks. However, even this recognition was circumscribed by a general reservation about the very idea of minorities in Bulgaria and the 1971 Constitution, unlike the 1947 Constitution, makes no specific references to ethnic minorities but rather refers to 'citizens of non-Bulgarian origin' (Article 45). Since 1985 the only recognized minorities in Bulgaria with their own minority organizations are the small number of Jews and the Armenians.

The 1965 census recorded 746,755 ethnic Turks, an increase of approximately 90,000 on the 1956 figure. Since then there have been no official figures for the total numbers of members of ethnic minorities in Bulgaria and in 1975 the section recording nationality on personal identity cards was reportedly removed.

Emigration

At various times since World War II, Bulgaria and Turkey have reached agreement over the emigration of Turks from Bulgaria to Turkey. The largest number of such emigrants left Bulgaria in the period 1949 to 1951. In August 1950 the Bulgarian government announced that a total of 250,000 Turks had applied to leave. The Turkish government, on the other hand, said it was unable to receive such a huge mass of people within such a short time and in November 1950 closed its border with Bulgaria because of 'illegal crossing of borders'. Two months later an agreement was reached by both governments that only those Turks who were in possession of a Turkish entry visa would be allowed to leave. Despite this agreement Bulgaria continued to evict Turks with the result that in November 1951 Turkey again closed its border. According to the Turkish authorities, Bulgaria had forged Turkish entry visas in order to rid itself of as many Turks as possible. However, some 155,000 left Bulgaria for Turkey in this period.

In 1968 a further agreement was reached which allowed the departure of close relatives of those who had left in the period 1944 to 1951. This agreement expired on 30 November 1978 and an announcement in the Sofia daily newspaper *Otechestven Front* of 2 August 1979 stated 'Since then between the two countries no agreement on emigration has existed.' The last official Bulgarian figure given for those who had emigrated under this agreement was 52,392 for the period up to August 1977 although Turkish sources state that some 130,000 left in total under the agreement.[15] From then until May 1989 emigration ceased except in a few individual cases of family reunification — such as when the Turkish authorities paid an estimated one million US dollars to the Bulgarian authorities to allow the emigration of the close relatives of the champion weight lifter Naim Suleymanoglu, who defected from Bulgaria in December 1986. Additionally a number of children, 64 in the period January 1987 to April 1988, both of whose parents had emigrated to Turkey were allowed to join them although there remained still a number of such cases outstanding. Leading Bulgarian officials categorically denied that emigration would be restarted. For example, Stanko Todorov, then member of the BCP Central Committee, Politburo and Chairman of the National Assembly, stated in a speech of 28 March 1985: 'there is not and will not be any emigration to Turkey' and that 'no Bulgarian/Turkish talks will be held in this connection'.[16] However the situation dramatically changed in May 1989.

Education and culture

In line with Marxist-Leninist theory, the first Constitution of the People's Republic of Bulgaria, adopted on 4 December 1947, contained provision for minority groups. For example, Article 71 stated that although the study of Bulgarian was obligatory in schools 'National minorities have a right to be educated in their vernacular, and to develop their vernacular, and to develop their national culture.'

There was also set up a Turkish language department at Sofia University as well as a number of Turkish language publications and schooling in Turkish. In 1964, on the 10th anniversary of one such Turkish publication, *Yeni Hayat*, Todor Zhivkov himself stated:

'All possible opportunities have been created for the Turkish population to develop their culture and language freely . . . The children of the Turkish population must learn their mother tongue and perfect it. To this end, it is necessary that the teaching of the Turkish language be improved in schools. Now and in the future the Turkish population will speak their mother tongue; they will write their contemporary literary works [in Turkish]; they will sing their wonderfully beautiful songs [in Turkish] . . . Many more books must be published in this country in Turkish, including the best works of progressive writers in Turkey.'

Turkish language schools were merged with Bulgarian schools and by the early 1970s the teaching of Turkish in Bulgarian schools had ceased. The Department of Turkish at Sofia University which reportedly attracted large numbers of students, of whom 70% were estimated to be ethnic Turks, stopped admitting students. In 1974 the whole department was shut down and replaced by a department for Arabic studies with new staff and only a few students — mostly apparently children of diplomatic staff stationed in Arab countries. If the aim of this was to prevent the formation of a Turkish intelligentsia which might lead a movement in the future for minority rights, this may have been counter-productive as ethnic Turks were forced to pursue other subjects which had better job prospects than, for example, philology in the old Turkish department.

After 1951 the Bulgarian government and BCP made attempts to integrate Turks into the state and party apparatus and large numbers were admitted into the BCP. However, there was constant criticism in official publications about their lack of party discipline and socialist consciousness. In 1971, the BCP programme which is still in force, stated that 'the citizens of our country of different national origins will come ever closer together'.[17] By the mid-1970s the use of the term 'unified Bulgarian socialist nation' became common parlance in official publications and speeches. In his speech of March 1985 (quoted above), Stanko Todorov categorically stated that Bulgaria was a 'one-nation state' and that in the 'Bulgarian nation there are no parts of any other peoples and nations'.

Ethnic Turks are reportedly unable to join the police force or make their career in the army and ethnic Turk conscripts serve in unarmed units engaged in national construction, for example building work after a couple of weeks rudimentary training with substitute weapons. The inference is that the Bulgarian authorities do not trust the ethnic Turks enough to train them properly in the army.

Population growth

The growth rate of the population in Bulgaria has been consistently decreasing in recent years. In 1980 the natural growth rate — that is the rate measured by the difference between the number of births and the number of deaths — was 3.6 per 1000, the lowest since records began. In 1981 it dropped to 2.8, in 1982 it dropped to 2.7 and in 1984 it was again down to 2.4 There have been a number of articles on this decline in the official press in recent years. The growth rates for the minorities — especially the ethnic Turks, the Pomaks, and the Gypsies — has been considerably higher than that for the majority of the population. This can be illustrated by comparing the official figures for specific areas, for example Lovech, Mihailovgrad and Vidin, all areas with negligible minority populations, with those that have a high proportion of minority populations, for example Blagoevgrad (where there are large numbers of Macedonians) and Smolyan (Pomaks) and Kardzhali (where there are concentrations of ethnic Turks).

The figures in Table 1 show that Lovech, Mihailovgrad and Vidin all have negative growth rates (that is the population is actually declining) and that this negative growth rate is increasing. The figures also highlight the continuous drift of the population from the countryside to the towns. The areas with large minorities, however, have higher than average growth rates, especially Kardzhali, and the drift to the towns is not so marked (and in the case of Kardzhali does not exist).

This highlights a double concern for the authorities. Firstly, the minority population is rapidly increasing while that of the majority is actually declining and, given the high birth rate of ethnic Turks, the actual figure for their number may well be in excess of the estimated 900,000 and is probably nearer to 15% than the more conservative estimate of 10% of the total population. Additionally, ethnic Turks are estimated to be a larger proportion of the work force, some 15-20% due to the high birth rate.

Secondly, large areas of the countryside, especially the important agricultural areas in the south around Kardzhali — vital for Bulgaria's valuable tobacco exports — and the Dobrudzha — a major wheat-growing region — are becoming increasingly populated by the minorities; so much so that before the campaign in 1984-5 it was possible to travel through large areas of Bulgaria without hearing Bulgarian spoken at all. The authorities concern is compounded in the case of the ethnic Turks living in the south near Smolyan and Kardzhali by the proximity of Turkey, so that while there was no apparent irredentist movement of any description before the name-changing campaign of 1984-5 such a movement arising in the future is not out of the question and the example of the growth of the ethnic Albanian population in Kosovo in Yugoslavia and the attendant problems for the Yugoslav authorities must be a worrying one for the Bulgarian government.

Religion

Both the Pomaks and the ethnic Turks (with the exception of the Gagauz, estimated to number a few thousand, who profess the Eastern Orthodox Christian faith and live near Varna in the north) are Sunni Muslim, while the Gypsies are estimated to be 75% Muslim and 25% Eastern Orthodox in religious adherence. As religion was until this century more important than language in differentiating between different groups, the Pomaks tended to feel greater affinity with the Turks than with Christian Bulgarians; similarly with the Muslim Gypsies (hence the second part of the proverb mentioned in the introduction). Ethnic Turks and Pomaks have often deliberately or otherwise been confused with each other and ethnic Turks were in many cases subjected to the same pressures as the Pomaks, especially where they inhabited the same village communities, to induce them to exchange their Muslim names for Bulgarian ones and, in effect, to renounce their religion and ethnic identity. This confusion between ethnic Turks and Pomaks has been deliberately used by the Bulgarian authorities which since the name-changing campaign of 1984/5 has consistently claimed that all ethnic Turks are Slav Bulgarians by descent who were forcibly islamicized by the Ottoman authorities, i.e. that they are all Pomaks.

Adherence to the Islamic faith was and is seen by the authorities as being a key factor inhibiting loyalty to the communist government. This was clearly set out in 1977 in an article in *Filosofska Misul* — an official publication published in Sofia. This article, which provides a valuable insight into the Bulgarian authorities' attitude to the Pomaks and to Muslims in general states:

'It was clear to the Bulgarian Communist Party that the Bulgarian Mohammedan problem was, above all, of social origin. That is why, following the 9 September 1944 victory of the socialist revolution, it set as its objective the elimination, above all, of the social roots of Islam in the Rhodope along with the age-old isolation and separation of Islamicized Bulgarians, to heal the wounds and traumas in their spirituality, to eliminate the division traced by the Turkish feudals, intensified by the Bulgarian bourgeoisie, to emancipate the Bulgarian awareness in them, dulled and concealed in the course of centuries, and to accelerate their joining the Bulgarian socialist nation.

However, in the Rhodope Islam has retained its strong positions in life and social mentality. Whereas it has already been "expelled" in the realm of social relations and the collectives, and in the social system of rituals and ceremonies, it clings adamantly and reproduces itself in family relations, holidays, and traditions. It is precisely for this reason that the new stage in the course of the cultural revolution in the Rhodope requires a more active interference in the way of life and in "expelling" Islam from the realm of family relations.

The struggle against Islamic fanaticism in the Rhodope and its derived tendency of alienation from what is Bulgarian is not a subjective requirement but an objective form of class and ideological struggle, and a reflection of the objective historical law of the consolidation of Islamicized Bulgarians within the Bulgarian socialist nation. The atheistic struggle in the Rhodope both presumes and encompasses the problem of breaking down the socio-political complex in the minds, behaviour, and way of life of a certain segment of the Bulgarian population and is interwoven with their class-party, patriotic, and internationalist education. A characteristic feature of the struggle for atheism in the Rhodope is that not only is it being deployed in the struggle against Islam but is also linked with the struggle for Bulgarian nationhood, and for the development of a new awareness, way of life, customs, and traditions. This presumes their cleansing from accumulated Islamic-Turkish influence.

The uncompromising struggle against Islam and its adverse consequences to some Rhodope Bulgarians is an important task at the present stage and a necessary prerequisite for their consolidation within the Bulgarian socialist nation and more active inclusion in building a developed socialist society.'

The rise of Islamic fundamentalism, the influence of the Iranian revolution of 1979, and the example of Lebanon —

Year	Lovech	Mihailovgrad	Vidin	Blagoevgrad	Smolyan	Kardzhali
1979	−2.8	−1.6	−4.8	+9.6	+9.9	+17.9
Towns	+4.5	+8.6	+8.4	+13.1	+12.0	+17.7
Villages	−10.9	−11.8	−17.9	+6.0	+7.7	+17.9
1981	−3.3	−3.3	−6.3	+9.3	+7.8	+15.9
Towns	+4.6	+5.9	+4.9	+10.9	+9.8	+12.7
Villages	−12.4	−13.3	−18.2	+7.4	+5.5	+17.3
1984	−4.6	−4.9	−7.2	+8.3	+7.7	+14.0
Towns	+3.6	+4.2	+4.4	+9.4	+9.5	+12.4
Villages	−14.9	−16.5	−21.1	+6.9	+5.5	+14.7

Table 1: Population growth per 1000 inhabitants

(Figures from *Statisticheski Godishnik na Narodna Republika Bulgaria*, 1980, 1982 and 1985)

relatively close to Bulgaria — have hardened the attitudes set out in this article although there is no apparent indication that there has been as yet a growth of Islamic fundamentalism within Bulgaria. However there is little doubt that the ethnic Turks have stronger religious leanings than ethnic Bulgarians as is illustrated in Tables 2 and 3.

The above figures show how religious attitudes have remained strong among the ethnic Turks, especially peasants, as compared to ethnic Bulgarians — a situation which is not to the liking of the authorities. An article in the daily newspaper *Rabotnichesko Delo* of 21 November 1984 spoke of 'the extreme aggressiveness of the ideological enemy, whose basic trump card is to play on the ethnic affiliations of part of the Rhodope population' and there have been a number of similar attacks against the penetration of Muslim influences into the country and against Islamic religious customs. For example, an article in the newspaper *Nova Svetlina* in June 1985 stated that fasting during the month of Ramadan was nothing but a 'destructive superstition' and an article in the newspaper *Otechestven Front* of 27 November 1984 referred to religious fanaticism still prevailing among 'Bulgarian Turks' and condemned those, especially in the Haskovo and Kardzhali districts, who raise families 'according to the dogmas of the Koran and the Muslim religion' without concluding civil marriages.

Modernization

Another factor in the assimilation campaign and one which is not prejudicial to the motives of the Bulgarian authorities is that of modernization. The BCP claims to be possessor of an ideology, Marxist-Leninism, which aims at the rapid implementation of policies to turn Bulgaria into a modern industrial state. Progress along these lines since the BCP took power after World War II has been, up till the present, impressive. The existence of a large minority, living in concentrated areas, speaking a completely different language (Turkish is an Asiatic language whilst Bulgarian is an Indo-European one) and 'clinging' to a traditional way of life is, perhaps inevitably, to be seen as an obstacle to the modernization process. In a modern state such as the one the BCP claims to be introducing it is essential for all citizens to speak a common language, in this case of course Bulgarian, and while Bulgarian has been compulsory in all schools many ethnic Turks, especially those living in areas where the majority of the population are ethnic Turks, learn only a basic Bulgarian and many older people speak it badly and some not at all.

Various Islamic customs such as fasting during the month of Ramadan are also seen by the authorities as being in contradiction to the precepts of modernization and articles in the official press have attacked these customs as being outdated in the era of factory discipline, etc. Thus both language and customs can be seen as obstacles in the path of modernization and the authorities claim that ethnic Turks, or 'Islamicized Bulgarians' as they are now officially referred to, have been offered the opportunity to become first class citizens like the majority population. (All these aspects are reflected in the above mentioned article from *Filosofska Misul*).

Identity cards and census

1985 was the last year of the five-year period for replacing all identity cards and a national census was scheduled to be held in December 1985. This may have been one of the factors in the intensity and short duration of the campaign to change all the names of the ethnic Turks from Islamic forms to Bulgarian ones.

Fear of assimilation by Turkey and the examples of Greece and Yugoslavia

The five centuries of Ottoman control have indelibly left their mark on the Bulgarian national psyche. The title of the most famous book by Bulgaria's most famous author, Ivan Vazov, is *Pod Igoto [Under the Yoke]* referring to this period and the symbolism of the yoke is universally used both officially and unofficially in this connection. As already noted the modern Bulgarian national awakening only occurred in the last century and was faced as much by the threat of Greek assimilation as Turkish. Throughout Eastern Europe fear of assimilation on the part of small nations is very real and examples like the Kashubs (a small Slavic people of northern Poland) which have effectively been assimilated over recent centuries are a warning to other small nations like the Bulgarian which is not greatly enlarging its population if at all. On its borders is the traditional enemy, Turkey, with a population of over 50 million and growing and within its own borders there is a large minority of Turks which are also growing at a rapid rate.

Compounding this situation are the examples of what has happened to the populations included in the San Stefano 'Greater Bulgaria' but which, apart from brief periods during the world wars, have been lost to Bulgaria. These are the Macedonians of Yugoslavia, Greece and Albania, and

---

Table 2: Religious attitudes (%)

	Bulgarians	Ethnic Turks
Active believers	5.72	12.50
Passive believers	11.38	33.75
Uncertain	21.82	11.80
Passive atheists	23.94	16.08
Active atheists	23.94	10.23

(From S. Tahirov, *Sotsialisticheska obrechnost i duhovno edinstvo*, Sofia, 1984)[18]

Table 3: Religious activity of ethnic Turks (%)

	Total	Workers	White-collar	Peasants
Mosque attendance	53.8	45.1	20.2	60.7
Weekly	11.4	5.1	3.6	14.8
Monthly	9.3	8.1	1.2	10.5
Festivals only	33.2	33.2	15.5	35.5
Non-attendance	45.9	54.6	79.8	39.9

(From M. Beytullov, 'Izmenie v religioznata praktika na Balgarskite Turtsi' in *Ateistichna Tribuna*, Sofia, 1976)[19]

San Stefano Bulgaria is still seen by most Bulgarians as what should have been (and should be).

The situation regarding the small number of Macedonians living in Albania is unclear due to the extreme secrecy of the Albanian authorities. Estimates of the number of Macedonians in Albania range from '3000 to 4000 distributed in nine villages of Prespa' — Enver Hoxha the then Albanian leader to the 7th Congress of the Albanian Labour Party in 1975 — to over 100,000 in a recent book published in Skopje in 1983.[20] This last figure appears to be exaggerated and most observers put the figure at 15,000-30,000. The abolishing of organized religion and the Law on First and Last Names in 1976 whereby all religious names and names which were not Albanian were to be replaced is seen by some Yugoslav observers as facilitating an alleged assimilation policy in Albania but lack of information makes such judgement impossible.

The situations in Greece and Yugoslavia however are much clearer. In Greece the large Slav-speaking population in Agean Macedonia has been successfully assimilated by a mixture of diluting the population with a massive influx of Greeks from Asia Minor after the population exchanges following the Greco-Turkish War of 1922, and an at times (especially under Metaxas in the late 1930s) severe discrimination similar to that now applied by the Bulgarian authorities to its own ethnic Turks. In Yugoslavia since World War II the Yugoslav authorities have apparently successfully nurtured a Macedonian national consciousness separate from the Bulgarian one by using the regional differences between the populations of Vardar Macedonia in Yugoslavia and those in Bulgaria. These differences have been amplified by creating a literary Macedonian language as far removed from Bulgarian as is feasible, by retrospectively retracing the new nation back through history, and by using the full power of the state bureaucracy and education system to instill the new consciousness into the population (see sections on Macedonia and Greece).

Partial assimilation up to December 1984

As noted above ethnic Turks and Pomaks have often, deliberately or otherwise, been confused with each other and where they cohabited in the same villages previous campaigns against the Pomaks to forcibly change their names have also included similar measures against ethnic Turks.

For example during army manoeuvres in early 1984, the village of Dolni Voden near Asenovgrad in the district of Plovdiv was reportedly surrounded by troops and the inhabitants, all ethnic Turks and Pomaks, were forced to change their names. In 1976 there were reports of demonstrations of Turks and Pomaks in the Plovdiv area protesting at discrimination against Muslims in employment and at the closing of several mosques.

A number of ethnic Turks in this period were charged with espionage apparently because of their opposition to official policy vis-à-vis the ethnic Turks. An example is Yusuf Husnu, an ethnic Turk from Varna, born in 1937 who was an agrarian economist and a member of the BCP. He held strong views on discrimination against ethnic Turks, particularly in matters of religion and freedom of opinion. He also had relatives living in Turkey and had made attempts to leave Bulgaria with his family. He was arrested in 1976 on charges of espionage and sentenced to 12 years' imprisonment in 1977. The charges of espionage appear to have been related to his alleged connections with a Turkish lorry driver. In 1984 he was released and allowed to emigrate to Turkey.[21]

Additionally, Turkish citizens, often former Bulgarian citizens who had emigrated to Turkey, have been similarly imprisoned for espionage or for 'anti-state agitation and propaganda' while visiting relatives in Bulgaria.

The pressures on the population can be seen by the contents of an official document dated 3 August 1984, relating to the municipality and regions around Stambolovo, south of Haskovo. The document, widely publicized outside Bulgaria, forbids the wearing of *shalvari* — traditional Turkish trousers — and the speaking of Turkish in the street, public places, and institutions. The order, signed by the mayor of Gledka states that those wearing *shalvari* or speaking Turkish will be refused service in shops and that only Bulgarian will be allowed to be spoken in kindergartens. In the light of later official statements denying the existence of a Turkish minority in Bulgaria, it is significant that the order refers to 'the Turkish population'.

Thus from the available information it appears that although there were certain instances of attempts at forcible assimilation of the ethnic Turkish minority, sometimes involving whole villages, this was not pursued by the authorities on a consistent countrywide basis before December 1984.

The name-changing campaign of December 1984 to March 1985

The situation radically changed in late 1984 when the Bulgarian authorities initiated a countrywide campaign to forcibly change the names of all ethnic Turks in Bulgaria. On the grounds that the roads were blocked due to adverse weather conditions, access to the regions where the ethnic Turks predominate was not allowed to foreign observers or visitors and these restrictions remained in force for certain areas, notably those around Kardzhali in the south and Yablanovo in the eastern Stara Planina until 1989.

After an initial period of complete silence in this matter which lasted until reports of the campaign began to appear in the news media outside Bulgaria in early 1985, the Bulgarian authorities stated that the ethnic Turks were in fact descendants of Slav Bulgarians who had been forcibly converted to Islam under Ottoman rule (i.e. that they were Pomaks). The authorities further stated that these 'Slav Bulgarians' were all 'voluntarily' and 'spontaneously' requesting new Bulgarian names as a sign of their 'rebirth in the Bulgarian nation'. The authorities have called this name-changing campaign 'the reconstruction of Bulgarian names' and have repeatedly denied that there has been any element of force or coercion involved. There is no doubt that some ethnic Turks did voluntarily request new names, especially those in the party/state apparatus but such cases were rare compared to the majority where these 'voluntary' and 'spontaneous' requests were made under severe duress.

The methods used by the authorities were similar to those used in the past against the Pomaks. Villages with predominately Turkish inhabitants were surrounded by police with dogs and troops with tanks, often in the early hours of the morning. Officials with new identity cards, or in other cases with a list of 'official' names to choose from, visited every household and the inhabitants were forced, in some cases at gun-point, to accept the new cards and to sign 'voluntary' forms requesting their new names. There are many reports of violence and rape by the security forces. In other instances the inhabitants of ethnic Turkish villages were assembled in the main square of the village where they were then obliged to accept the new identity cards.

In villages with mixed populations, for example Preslavets near Harmanli in Haskovo district whose population is approximately 50% Turkish, similar methods were used by the authorities. However in areas where the ethnic Turkish population constitutes only a small minority of the population, especially in cities, the operation was more low-key. For example in Harmanli itself which has a population of 25,000 to 30,000 with at most 1000 ethnic Turkish inhabitants, the name-changing and the issuing of new identity cards were carried out at the work-place, and in some instances ethnic Turks were given a period of days to accept the new cards or else lose their jobs.

The campaign began in the southern regions of the country in December 1984 and then steadily worked northwards reaching around Varna and the Dobrudzha in the north-east by January/February 1985. By the end of March the operation had apparently been completed and Stanko Todorov, then Chairman of the National Assembly, in a speech of 28 March 1985 reported that the 'resumption' of Bulgarian names by citizens with 'Turkish-Arabic' names had been 'completed safely', stressing that Bulgaria was a 'one-nation state' and that in the 'Bulgarian nation there are no parts of any other people and nations'. This operation had, he said, taken place 'speedily, spontaneously and calmly'.[22]

Other aspects of the assimilation campaign

Religion and religious customs

Article 53, paragraph 1, of the Bulgarian Constitution guarantees freedom of conscience and creed to citizens who also 'may perform religious rites'. The same paragraph also allows 'anti-religious propaganda' and as noted above the authorities have attacked Islamic traditions and Islam in general with growing frequency in official publications over a long period. Paragraph 2 of the same article states that 'the church shall be separated from the state'. In practice, however, all religious officials are paid by the state and the state is responsible for the preservation and maintenance of all churches and mosques.

Since the campaign of December 1984 there have been a number of reports of mosques forcibly closed or destroyed although the number which have been actually destroyed is apparently small. These include the mosque in Gorski Izvor near the border with Greece which was forcibly closed by officials on 15 January 1985; the minaret destroyed and the building turned into a tobacco warehouse; and one of the two mosques in Haskovo, the minaret of which was destroyed at the end of 1986. More common has been the practice of closing local mosques and ostensibly turning them into museums usually with the sign 'Museum of Bulgarian Mussulmen' on the locked doors. The half-crescent habitually found on the top of minarets has in most instances been removed, apparently as being too associated with the Turkish national symbol.

According to a report by one of the very few foreign journalists allowed by the authorities to visit areas where ethnic Turks predominate since the campaign began, Islamic clerics who voluntarily changed their names were granted a salary increase in January 1985 of 50 leva ($50), making their total salary about 200 leva per month. The same source asserted that mosques in Bulgaria have been divided into two categories: 'official' and 'non-official'. 'Official' mosques are those which have an 'official' imam recognized as such by the authorities, that is those where the local imam has cooperated with the authorities in the name-changing campaign. Mosques in the other category of 'non-official' mosques have been closed.[23]

Another journalist who visited Bulgaria was the Turkish journalist Kamil Taylan. He was given special permission by

the Bulgarian authorities to make a film report within Bulgaria in September 1986 for West German television apparently because of his left wing stance and previous criticism of Turkey. His experiences demonstrate the constraints imposed even upon journalists whom the Bulgarian authorities might view as sympathetic. He was permanently accompanied by 'guides' who refused to let him use the term Turks but rather 'reborn Bulgarian Muslims'. He was also strongly discouraged from conducting interviews in Turkish although in practice this was often unavoidable as some of the subjects for interview knew no other language. He was also refused permission to visit Kardzhali, one of the main ethnic Turkish areas, and the authorities admitted to him that there had been violent clashes between security forces and demonstrators against the name-changing campaign in Haskovo. Despite these and many other restrictions he was able, often in conversation when he had succeeded in temporarily losing his 'guide', to compile much information, especially regarding the religious aspect of the assimilation campaign.

He was allowed to visit Shumen, an ethnic Turkish area in the north-east of the coutry. There he was informed: that the authorities had replaced the previous *mufti* who had reportedly opposed the name-changing campaign, with one who would support the authorities' assimilation campaign; that young people were not allowed to go to mosque and that those who tried faced harassment and possible arrest; that all religious classes and teachings of the Koran in mosques was forbidden; that circumcision of male infants was strictly forbidden and that those who had this operation performed were imprisoned; and that all separate Muslim cemeteries have been abolished. The number of mosques in Shumen had been reduced to three, with seven others demolished in the preceding years and from January 1987 the main mosque in Shumen would be closed for restoration, apparently for some years.

Kamil Taylan also visited Plovdiv where again he was informed that young people faced arrest if they attempted to go to mosques which were open only for prayers on Fridays at noon. There an *imam* informed him that 'There are two mosques left in Filibe [Plovdiv] district. We are imams without mosques. We are paid a salary for show. They gather us to show to delegations like yours from other countries to prove that religion is free.' The imam also told Taylan not to believe what the mufti of Plovdiv told him stating that 'he is definitely their man'.

From this and many other such reports by refugees and others it appears that Islamic religious practice is, while not completely banned, severely curtailed and that only old people are allowed to pray in the few mosques left open and then only once a week. It would appear that the Bulgarian authorities are not prepared to unduly antagonize Islamic world opinion by an outright ban as this would jeopardize foreign relations with a number of currently friendly Arab states, for example Syria whose Grand Mufti visited Sofia in July 1985 and declared that he was satisfied that there was religious freedom in Bulgaria for Muslims. Less convinced was the delegation from the Organization of Islamic Countries led by Abdullah Omar Nasif of Saudi Arabia which visited Bulgaria in 1987, and the UN Special Rapporteur on Religious Intolerance for the Human Rights Committee, Angelo Vidal D'Almeido who named Bulgaria as one of seven countries systematically preventing the peaceful practice of religion.[24]

On 6 March 1985 the Bulgarian authorities publicized a letter signed by leading Islamic officials with their new Bulgarian names. The signatories were the Chief Mufti, the regional mufti for Plovdiv (who also signed as 'interim in charge of the mufti of Kardzhali' which meant that at the time there was no mufti for Kardzhali — the district where most of the major demonstrations by ethnic Turks had taken place), and the regional muftis for Shumen, Tolbuhin, Razgrad, Smolyan and Aytos. This letter denied that the practice of Islamic religious rites had in any way been infringed.

Despite this and other public assurances of freedom to practice Islam and events like the appearance of the mufti of Plovdiv at a press conference held for foreign journalists in Sofia on 6 February 1985 to counter allegations of his death, it is obvious that there has been some opposition from imams against the religious restrictions. As noted above the mufti of Shumen was replaced apparently due to his opposition to the assimilation policy and in July 1988 the mufti was again replaced apparently because the new man also was not sufficiently amenable to the authorities' policies — when asked outright by a western diplomat in the presence of Bulgarian officials whether the allegations concerning the assimilation campaign were true or not, he had answered by an eloquent silence. On 11 November the Chief Mufti, Mirian Topchiev, was replaced but this is not seen as due to his opposition. The new Chief Mufti is Nedyo Gendzhev who from 1986 to 1988 was regional mufti of Kardzhali and therefore undoubtably loyal to the new policy.

Other local imams have been arrested, like Yusein Kabov of Gorski Izvor, and in at least one other case allegedly killed. Enbiye Omerov Mahmudov, the Imam of Podayva village near Razgrad was, according to the Turkish newspaper *Milliyet* killed by security forces. The Bulgarian journal *Nova Svetlina* on 11 June 1985 published an article purporting to refute this claim and showed a picture of a man named Biser Albenov, who said that he had been imam of Podayva for 15 to 20 years and denied any human rights violations had occurred during the name-changing campaign. The article strongly implied that Enbiye Omerov Mahmudov was now named Biser Albenov and was alive and well. However a relative of Enbiye Mahmudov, who also lived in Podayva before emigrating to Turkey, states that the man in the photograph had not been imam prior to the name-changing campaign and that his name had been Basri Ahmedov Mollamedov and that he had been employed in the peasant cooperative in Podayva and was not imam prior to the campaign. The same source asserts that Enbiye Mahmudov was killed by the security forces. Further confusion is spread by the fact that *Nova Svetlina* in the same article states that the regional mufti from Razgrad is called Ilia Dimitrov when all other official publications, including the above-mentioned letter of 6 March 1985 by the muftis, name him as Ilia Georgiev.

Official pressure on religious figues has continued. On 11 May 1989 there was a meeting of imams with the Chief Mufti where they were once again told to only use Bulgarian in all religious services and in general conversation, or face punishment. The imams were further informed about a forthcoming visit by a foreign delegation (believed to be a delegation from the Parliamentary Assembly of the Council of Europe which was due to visit Bulgaria on 13 July 1989) and that they were to say that they were happy with their lives, suffered no religious restrictions, and that there was no problem during the name-changing campaign. The imams were warned that government officials would be accompanying the delegation and any imam who did not follow these instructions would be punished.

Despite such public assurances of freedom to practice Islam as the muftis' letter, there have been many official attacks on Islamic practices especially the circumcision of male infants. The position regarding circumcision of the small but officially recognized Jewish community in Bulgaria whose religion also calls for circumcision of male infants is unclear, however there is no ambiguity regarding the ethnic Turks. Georgi Tanev, First Secretary of the Kardzhali District Party Committee, stated in a speech on 15 May 1985 in Kardzhali, that 'Turkish reactionary forces in their subversive anti-Bulgarian propaganda in connection with the process of rebirth [i.e. the name-changing campaign] rely first of all on the religion of Islam'. He went on to call for the total abolition of circumcision and for 'energetic measures' to be taken against 'all those involved, and (that) the parents who allow it, all those who carry out or assist circumcision should be held strongly responsible'.[25] This speech is typical of many by party activists in the period April to August 1985.

In practice this meant that the authorities made periodic checks on the population to make sure that male children were not being circumcised. In early 1985 in the south of the country some parents were obliged to sign forms stating that prosecution under Article 324(2) in connection with Article 20(2) of the Criminal Code would result if their sons were circumcised. Article 324(2) deals with practising a profession connected with public health without suitable qualifications or permission and Article 20(2) deals with instigating a crime. People convicted under this legislation face punishment of up to three years' imprisonment or a fine of up to 1000 leva (US$1000).

Although Bulgarian officials have reportedly stated that circumcision is illegal only if performed by untrained people outside the medical profession and that circumcision is freely available in hospital under proper medical supervision, in practice this is not the case and the authorities have heavily penalized those involved in circumcision. Initially fathers whose children were found to have been circumcised since the last monthly check were imprisoned as were the doctors who performed the operation. However, this was apparently not enough to deter the population and in 1986 the pressure was stepped up by imprisoning mothers and even grandmothers, reportedly for up to five years. The repressive measures seem to have been successful and circumcision of male infant Turks has by all accounts ceased.

The authorities have also attacked the practice of fasting in *Ramadan* and have attempted to stop the traditional celebrations of *Bayram* when the head of the household traditionally slaughters a sheep, even going as far as searching houses during Bayram in the Kardzhali district and searching refrigerators for sheep's carcasses. In August/ September 1986 a 49-year-old man was imprisoned for one year after such a search found a sheep in his refrigerator.

The Islamic custom of washing the body of the deceased prior to burial has also been forbidden and separate Muslim cemeteries have been abolished with many such cemeteries destroyed and the headstones smashed, e.g. the Turkish cemetery in Ardino which was flattened by heavy plant machinery at the beginning of 1986.

Language and traditional clothes

As noted above all schooling in Turkish ceased by the mid-1970s. At the 23rd session of UNESCO's general conference on 14 October 1985, Academician Blagovest Sendov, replying to a statement made by a member of the Turkish delegation, stated that emigration to Turkey had 'objectively eliminated the need for instruction in a language [Turkish] which is alien to the Bulgarian nationals'. However there were a number of official Turkish-language publications which ceased during the name-changing campaign. For example, the bilingual publication *Nova Svetlina* (Bulgarian) or *Yeni Isik* (Turkish) was available only in Bulgarian after January 1985.

In association with the name-changing campaign there was a blanket ban on the speaking of Turkish in all public places on pain of a summary fine. The amount of the fine initially varied from five to 10 leva but has steadily increased since early 1985 to a fine of 50 to 100 leva for a first offence; one month's salary if repeated, followed by dismissal from work or even reported imprisonment of up to two years. All Turkish music has been banned and similar punishments are meted out to those caught listening to Turkish radio or listening to Turkish music cassettes with the additional punishment of confiscation of the radio or cassette player.

On 14 October 1986, during a visit by an Amnesty International delegation, Bulgarian embassy officials in Bonn, West Germany, claimed that the widely reported ban on the speaking of Turkish was 'nonsense' because 'there are old people who don't speak Bulgarian'. Referring to the official document signed by the Mayor of Gledka (see section on pre-1984 developments) banning the use of Turkish in public places on pain of 'sanctions', the officials admitted that 'some mayors' had initially made 'mistakes' but that this had been quickly rectified. However further documents contradict this. For example, Order No.144 dated 9 July 1986, issued by the director of the Cherno More mine in Burgas, explicitly forbids the speaking of Turkish throughout the entire mine complex and on the buses to and from the mine on pain of a fine.

Women wearing shalvari (traditional Turkish trousers) or other ethnic clothing are harassed in the street and also face fines. A document dated 20 September 1985 relates to all villages in Kardzhali district and is a standard letter from the mayor to all heads of families in the villages. This document states:

'In accordance with Article 2 of Order No.1 of the (village name) People's Communal Council, it is prohibited to wear shalvari, pyjamas, veils, *yashmaks* [traditional Islamic veils] and other non-traditional Bulgarian clothes or to speak a non-Bulgarian language in a public place. This tradition, inherited from five harsh centuries of slavery, has been forever rejected by the whole people, including the Muslims. Therefore we remind you that the time has come to end conservative modes of life and to adopt more appropriate and pleasant clothing and the pure Bulgarian tongue. We hereby warn that after 7 October those who do not abide by these requirements will be sanctioned.'

Employment and education

In the initial phases of the campaign, ethnic Turks who had not 'voluntarily' changed their names were not allowed to work in state enterprises, neither were they allowed to use their old names in any contact with the all-pervading state bureaucracy — for example they could not draw money out of the banks etc. without using their new names. As noted above such measures were often used as an alternative to brute force to induce ethnic Turks to change their names. A document dated 16 January 1985 relating to the Asenova Krepost works in Asenovgrad, south of Plovdiv, illustrates this. This document, Order No.21, states that all work forms, travel cards, sick records and other administrative documents have to be filled out with 'reconstructed Bulgarian names' and that 'all those with Arabic names who do not produce the necessary documents for name-changing will not be admitted for work'. The order also forbids the use of Turkish in work places.

It is not surprising that the Bulgarian authorities have not neglected the vital area of education in pursuing the assimilation campaign. Many ethnic Turkish teachers who were seen as unreliable by the authorities have been replaced and often sent into manual labour instead like Ziya Osmanov, the school director in Kroyachevo, and his brother Selhattin Osmanov, a geography teacher, both of whom were sacked

and sent to be miners in Maden. An official document dated 7 May 1985 from the District People's Council of Varbishta states that Sevda Rafailova Ognyanova, an ethnic Turk formerly named Saver Rifat Ahmetova, was relieved from her position, held since 1979, as director of a school in Lovets village, Shumen region, due to her attitude to the 'rebirth process' — this despite her acknowledged worth as a teacher and diligence in her job, and her membership of the BCP since 1975. The scale of replacement was particularly high in the south around Kardzhali in 1985. However, it appears from speeches made at the National Party Conference held on 28/29 January 1988 and reported in *Rabotnichesko Delo* on 31 January that the authorities were finding it hard to keep such specialists who had been sent into Muslim areas on double salaries in 1985 to bring the 'patriotic revolution' there, from leaving these areas.

Despite these apparent setbacks major emphasis has been made within the secondary school system and *Nova Svetlina* on 15 November 1988 reported on sessions organized in the schools at which pupils met 'Bulgarians' who have returned from living in Turkey to describe their 'bitter experiences' in 'capitalist Turkey' and their feelings of gratitude to be back in Bulgaria and to have rediscovered their 'true' national identities.

In addition there have been formed numerous geneological, folklore and local historical societies which aim to involve the Muslim population, especially school children, in programmes to indoctrinate them. For example *Nova Svetlina* on 23 February 1988 described how the Koleduvane folklore society in Razgrad, one of the main ethnic Turkish areas, had 'revived' traditional celebrations of Christmas among local Muslims.

Thus it can be seen that the Bulgarian authorities are using the education system in the scheme to attempt to eradicate a Turkish identity over a matter of a few generations. This time scale is confirmed by an article from a Razgrad newspaper, *Novo Ludogorie*, on 18 June 1987 which said that full assimilation of Bulgaria's Muslims would be achieved 'in several decades — a short historical period'.

Opposition by ethnic Turks

Resistance to the name-changing campaign

Major demonstrations against the name-changing campaign took place in a number of places. In Benkovski, a town in Kardzhali district near the border with Greece, according to eye-witness accounts, on 24 December 1984 demonstrators numbering some thousands of ethnic Turks from neighbouring villages and including women and children, marched to the town hall which was protected by 20 to 30 members of the elite special security forces known as the 'red berets' after their distinctive headgear. The security forces initially fired into the air above the crowd in an attempt to make them disperse. When this failed they fired into the ground in front of the advancing demonstrators who began to attack them and tried to disarm them. The security forces then opened fire into the crowd at point blank range, killing at least six including a two-year-old child and wounding 40.

Eyewitnesses described a similar demonstration which took place outside Momchilgrad Town Hall on or about 27 December 1984. These reports state that initially army units supported by tanks attempted to stop a large crowd of ethnic Turks, again including women and children, from approaching the town hall. When this failed, 'Red Beret' security forces attacked the demonstrators with iron truncheons covered in rubber. The crowd retaliated and attempted to storm the town hall, breaking some windows and tearing up pictures of Todor Zhivkov (the Bulgarian leader). The security forces then used water canon on the crowd, the majority of whom dispersed. Those who did not disperse were arrested. The authorities apparently photographed the demonstrators and a number of people suspected of being organizers were subsequently arrested. A strict curfew was imposed. On 1 April 1988, Stefan Solakov, a journalist who has written a number of pamphlets strongly denying any human rights abuses (e.g. *Dangerous Play* and *The Investigation*) for the official news agency Sofia Press, reportedly told a Reuters correspondent that 40 people including 10 militia members had died in a series of clashes in and around Momchilgrad in December 1984 and January 1985 when ethnic Turks confronted the authorities in protest at the name-changing campaign. Solakov reportedly stated that the militia had used water canon and tear gas against the demonstrators and that most of the victims had been crushed to death, apparently in a stampede that ensued. However this report was almost immediately denied by the Bulgarian Foreign Ministry and Solakov himself subsequently denied making the statements.[26]

Other violent demonstrations apparently involving loss of life are reported to have taken place in a number of places including: Gorno Prahovo; Mlechino, involving ethnic Turkish inhabitants from Gorno Prahovo and Dolno Prahovo as well as Mlechino; Dzhebel; and Ivaylovgrad near the border with Turkey where, according to an embassy official at the Bulgarian embassy in Bonn, three 'Muslims' (i.e. ethnic Turks) were killed by the security forces during a demonstration against the name-changing campaign when a crowd again attacked the town hall.[27]

Information on these and other reported violent incidents are hard to come by and the exact number of deaths is impossible to accurately assess. However it appears that most of the violent demonstrations took place in the southern regions of the country where the campaign began and that mass organized demonstrations were not so prevalent in the north as reports of how the authorities had dealt with such demonstrations spread ahead of the actual campaign. Violent clashes were reported however in Razgrad district.

The campaign reached the Stara Planina — the central mountain range — in late January/early February 1985 and it was here that perhaps the most spectacular event of the whole campaign took place — the three day siege of Yablanovo in the eastern Stara Planina. According to a participant in the siege, Mustafa Suleymanov, the inhabitants of the ethnic Turkish town of Yablanovo comprising of about 1500 households or some 6000 people, had received reports of the events in December 1984 in Momchilgrad and other places. As a result the inhabitants along with some ethnic Turks from nearby villages including Vrani Kon, Obitel, Filaretevo and Velichka, erected barricades around the town when the authorities arrived on 18 January 1985 to implement the campaign.

Virtually all the inhabitants of the town were ethnic Turks including the mayor, two of the three local policemen, and other officials many of whom, such as the mayor, were involved in the resistance and used official vehicles to bring in wood for the barricades and for the five or six fires which were lit in the town square by the town hall to warn the inhabitants who congregated there for the three days and nights of the siege despite the 20 cm. of snow and extreme cold.

The main entry to Yablanovo is from Kotel and the south-east and a barricade was erected in Malo Selo — a small village on the outskirts of the town. There was also a plan to use explosives from a quarry to destroy the bridge over the river Ticha at the entry to the town but in the event this did not happen. In order to prevent any informers in the village and also to prevent the police station from communicating with the authorities outside the town, the telephone wires were cut underground before the first house — one of the policemen's — on entering the town. The authorities had confiscated all hunting rifles a week previously and had removed all number plates of private cars to prevent the inhabitants from getting away. However some inhabitants made molotov cocktails and armed themselves with sticks and stones.

For three days the authorities (at this time mostly police and civilians) attempted to reason with the demonstrators to peacefully disperse but to no avail and on the fourth morning troops with tanks and other armoured vehicles using tear gas and live ammunition forced their way in. One of the main tank training schools for the Bulgarian army is located in nearby Sliven but Suleymanov gained the impression that troops had been especially drafted in from other regions of Bulgaria and noticed that the number plates of some of the vehicles used were from Kyustendil district.

How many people were killed or injured in the ensuing violence is hard to assess. One report states that 34 were killed and 29 or 30 taken to Kotel hospital — the nearest — with gunshot wounds. Suleymanov stated that he personally saw one man shot in both legs and heard of other deaths and estimated that perhaps six or seven had died but could not be sure as he escaped on the fourth morning for Sofia. All reports state that hundreds were arrested including one of the policemen, Ismail Alzhikov, and the mayor, Hyuseyin Nuhov, whose post was filled by a Bulgarian as were all other official posts in the town, even in the shops. Others arrested included Musa Musov, a teacher at the local primary school, and Fedal Fedalov, another senior official in the town. Many reports stated that the houses of some of the ringleaders were bulldozed but Suleymanov denies this and according to him the most serious material damage was that a number of gardens including trees in them were destroyed by the advancing tanks. The mosque was locked up and entry forbidden but it was not destroyed.

Suleymanov himself, previously a photographer for the originally bilingual (Turkish and Bulgarian) official publication *Nova Svetlina* (*Yeni Isik* or *New Light*), had left Yablanovo on the fourth morning of the siege and gone to Sofia with 156 petitions from households in the town protesting at the compulsory name-changing. He left a copy of the petition at the Public Prosecutors office in Sofia and was then arrested and taken to Sofia Central Prison. The next morning he was transferred to Sliven Central Prison where he was detained for one and a half months. Sliven Central Prison was so overcrowded with ethnic Turkish prisoners, 90% of whom he estimated were from Yablanovo, that some had to be held in garages. He was interrogated and severely punched, kicked and beaten with rubber truncheons and officially charged with resisting the state and inciting the populace. However he constantly pleaded forgiveness and was released without trial. Many of the others arrested were tried under Article 325 of the Criminal Code dealing with 'hooliganism' and sentenced to up to four years' imprisonment. Suleymanov was allowed to return to Yablanovo where, in his own words, he kept a very low profile and managed on 3 April 1985 to get on an official trip out of Bulgaria, first to Romania and then to the USSR where he applied for political asylum at the Turkish Embassy in Moscow. After 913 days at the embassy he was eventually allowed to go to Turkey. The Bulgarian authorities claim that he was a Turkish spy.

Assessing the number of ethnic Turks arrested during the name-changing campaign is extremely difficult and only vague estimates can be made. A Bulgarian who was detained in mid-1985 in Belene (a prison camp on an island in the Danube which was notorious in the 1950s for holding large numbers of political prisoners and where most ethnic Turks detained during the name-changing campaign were reportedly held) stated that there were at that time in Camp Number 2 of Belene 450 ethnic Turks detained there in connection with the campaign. Other reports agree with this estimate that there were in early 1985 in the entire camp complex of Belene about 1000 ethnic Turks. Many of these were apparently released after a period of some months without trial often followed by several years forced internal exile. Others were tried, often on charges of 'hooliganism' and sentenced to up to four years' imprisonment. Yet others were tried with more serious charges of espionage or 'Anti-state agitation' and received longer prison terms.

In 1987 there was a mass hunger strike of ethnic Turkish detainees in Belene and some were subsequently removed to other places of detention, especially the penal mine in Bobovdol. By late 1988 it was reported that few detainees remained in Belene and that those who had been tried and sentenced had been removed to normal prisons like Stara Zagora prison where most political prisoners are held.

In addition to the large numbers of people imprisoned and even killed, many ethnic Turks, including whole families, have been subjected to the administrative measure of internal banishment for protesting at the assimilation campaign. Under the terms of the 'People's Militia Law of 1976' Article 39(1), amended 12 August 1983, the authorities can, among other measures, apply without trial the 'preventive administrative measure' of 'compulsory residence in another place of habitation for a period of one to three years' on people who 'carry out anti-social activities affecting the security of the country'. These measures were often used as a supplementary punishment on ethnic Turkish prisoners after their release from Belene. Although such measures, which can be renewed indefinitely, cannot legally be applied to people under the age of 18, in some cases they have been used against whole families including young children.

This internal banishment of dissenting ethnic Turks has been tacitly admitted by the Bulgarian authorities. In a speech of 28 March 1985, Stanko Todorov, then a member of the BCP Central Committee Politburo and Chairman of the National Assembly, after denying categorically that there would be any emigration to Turkey, stated that all those 'who dance to the tune of Ankara's propaganda and her nationalist agents in Bulgaria' and who 'do not wish to live in their native towns and villages can move out'. For cases of this kind, he added, instructions had been given to the appropriate Bulgarian organs to ensure speedy removal (reportedly within hours), 'not to Turkey but to other regions of Bulgaria, where these people will be able to live peacefully and happily'.[28] Such internal banishment had been similarly used in the past against the Macedonians and the Pomaks.

Protests against the campaign were also made by many leaders of the Turkish community in Bulgaria. Ethnic Turkish students at Sofia University held a protest meeting at the end of December 1984 but participants faced arrest and imprisonment. Other reports state that certain well-known ethnic Turks who the authorities saw as potential leaders of resistance were detained in advance. During the actual campaign leaders faced imprisonment or worse; for example, Nedzhattin Eminov, a mathematics teacher from Ardino who was also a high-ranking official of the local branch of the Communist Party. According to an eyewitness account he was shot in the head twice in Studen Kladenets quarter of Kardzhali and buried on 17 July 1985 in Ardino. His apparent assassination was allegedly due to his position as a

leading member of the ethnic Turkish minority and his open espousal of nationalist views which had made him something of a leader for young ethnic Turks who opposed the name-changing campaign.

Other protest came from ethnic Turks holding high state posts, like Halil Ahmedov Ibishev, who at the time was a member of the Bulgarian National Assembly. Ibishev, now resident in Turkey, states:

'By the end of December 1984 rumours were spreading that the names of Turks living in the Kardzhali and Momchilgrad regions had been changed. Since it was said that these names were changed by force, the people in my constituency in Dalgopol asked me what was going on; so I conveyed their concerns to the Dalgopol Municipal Party Committee. The First Secretary of the party branch told me, "Don't worry – the changing of names does not apply to all Turks, only to Turkish women marrying Bulgarians". Later on I learned the horrifying facts. Bulgarian police and soldiers were raiding Turkish villages and assaulting the women. Some Turks had escaped to the mountains . . .

The main assault began in Kardzhali province in late December 1984. All the villages and cities where Turks lived were besieged by the military and police. It was forbidden for Turks to move in or out of the region. Anyone violating this would be taken to prison or killed. Then the campaign moved to other areas. Many houses were searched during the night, and many people tortured. The villages were besieged by tanks, military trucks, even fire trucks to ensure the completion of the name-changing campaign. Telephone conversations were interrupted, and it was made impossible for those in one Turkish village to phone other villages. You could not travel from one village to the next even by foot. In some areas the name-changing campaign was completed very quickly, in a couple of days, although it took longer in Kardzhali. Before the name-changing campaign got underway, young people and others who might fight the new policy were taken and put in special camps. There whereabouts were not known for 40 to 50 days. The schools were used as military headquarters. Anyone who asked questions or objected was taken away, and tortured.

The oppression came to our district in January 1985. The village filled with soldiers and police. Then I was called to the party committee and informed: "Turkish and Arab names will be changed to Bulgarian ones. You, as a Deputy and Representative of the people, will help us. You will explain that anybody who resists will be killed like a dog." I asked who had ordered this, and they replied that the Bulgarian Communist Party Central Committee had made the decision.

So on 24 January they began to change the names. They . . . banned the speaking of Turkish and stopped Turkish language radio broadcasts, Turkish tombstones were taken down.

A month or two after the name-changing campaign had been completed, circumcision was banned altogether. All children were examined, and it was recorded who had and who had not been circumcised. After that time, it was decreed that no further circumcisions could be carried out. Moreover, the examinations became periodic affairs, in order to ensure that circumcision was not carried out. And after the date when circumcision was banned, if a child was found to have been circumcised, his parents and the doctor who performed the operation were fined or imprisoned. Also, anyone else who aided the ceremony was punished. From my own village there was the case of a young man who travelled to another village to bring the man who would do the circumcision. This man was arrested and kept in prison 40 to 50 days, and he was still in prison when I escaped. It is just one example; there have been many similar cases.

At the end of 1984 at the time of the campaign in the south but before it reached my village, I requested to meet Todor Zhivkov [the Bulgarian leader] but this was refused. However I met Grisha Filipov [the then Prime Minister] and told him of the reports of force being used and asked him what would happen if we asked questions in the National Assembly and whether we could defend the rights of the ethnic Turks. Filipov replied that this was a question beyond the jurisdiction of our parliament and that the decision had been taken by the Politburo of the BCP and he warned me to avoid this problem and to keep silent, otherwise "you'll have problems with your family".'

Halil Ibishev also gives details of how he and other leading members of the ethnic Turkish minority had been forced to sign the open letter to Turgat Ozal, the Turkish Prime Minister, dated 27 November 1985[29] protesting at 'systematic attempts to interfere' into 'the internal affairs of our country' which was widely published by Sofia Press and distributed by Bulgarian embassies in a number of countries:

'I was invited to Sofia to the National Council of the Fatherland Front building in Sofia. There I met before the meeting 40 to 50 other members of the Turkish intelligentsia who like myself had no inkling about what was going to happen. After we had entered, Kamen Kalinov, an ethnic Turk formerly named Fahrettin Halilov and who was the Director in Chief of *Nova Svetlina*, informed us that there was a political campaign against the Bulgarian state mostly led by Ozal and that we all knew that all Turks had willingly changed their names and so to prove this we all have to sign the letter. The letter was then read out by Hristo Marinov, formerly Hamdi Mustafov, a secretary of the Fatherland Front, and we were all advised that anyone against the policy would be put in prison, lose their jobs or be deported. Nobody said anything and we all signed. The meeting was over in, at most, 45 minutes and I immediately left Sofia.

I was also invited to go on television and make a speech in favour of the new policy. I refused. After having refused I was told by a member of the District Committee of the Varna BCP, Vasil Rusev, who was also President of the District Committee of the Fatherland Front: "you are a member of parliament, you refused to speak on television but don't forget that if you continue to refuse your title will be cancelled and you maybe will not see your children and family again. Be careful from now on and act according to government policy".'

Another ethnic Turk who signed this open letter to Ozal was Naim Suleymanov — the world champion weightlifter who defected on 12 December 1986 during a sporting competition in Australia. On 13 December BTA claimed that it was suspected that he had been 'the victim of a terrorist act' and on 15 December BTA announced that he had been kidnapped and that the 'Shalamanov Operation [his new "Bulgarian" name was Naum Shalamanov] had been masterminded by the Turkish secret services, not without help of their colleagues in other countries'. Naim Suleymanov has since publicly stated that he left Bulgaria of his own free will because of the forced assimilation of the ethnic Turkish minority to which he belonged. On 24 January 1987 BTA announced that he had 'been treated with psychotropic drugs to induce his anti-Bulgarian statements'. This announcement by BTA followed publication of a number of press reports, quoting Suleymanov stating 'they changed our names at the end of 1984. In the District of Kardzhali 80-100 Turks were killed. Many were thrown in jail . . . The mosques were closed. Speaking Turkish was banned.' The close relatives of Naim Suleymanov (now called Naim Suleymanoglu) were allowed to emigrate and join him on 14 October 1988 after the Turkish government had paid a fee reportedly over one million US dollars to the Bulgarian government — Suleymanoglu was by this time a Turkish national hero after winning a gold medal for Turkey at the Seoul Olympics.

Another ethnic Turkish athlete who was not so fortunate is Byunyamin Manchev, a wrestler from Plovdiv. On 8 May 1985, the Turkish Broadcasting Authority broadcast a television interview with him recorded secretly in Budapest, Hungary, during an international tournament in which he was taking part. Manchev, apparently unaware that he was being filmed secretly, described how he and his family had been forced to change their names and alleged that ethnic Turks including children had been killed during the operation by the security forces. On 22 May 1985, however, BTA released a statement alleging that the interview with Manchev had been 'faked', and reported that in a written letter to BTA he stated that he had only spoken of rumours he had heard from Radio Free Europe. However, on 24 January 1987, he and his wife, his brother and uncle and their wives visited the home of a Turkish consular official in Plovdiv requesting permission to emigrate to Turkey. On leaving the house they were arrested and beaten. Manchev was subsequently sentenced to one year's imprisonment and on release sent into exile to Nova Mahala near Pazardzhik where his wife and children had also been exiled. His brother and uncle and their wives were also exiled to different parts of the country.

Many ethnic Turks fled to the mountains in the first phases of the campaign but adverse weather conditions made such flight not a long-term possibility. Many others attempted to leave the country — some managed to cross the heavily guarded border with Greece, many more made the easier route to Yugoslavia, and yet others even managed to escape via Romania and then to Yugoslavia. Those unfortunate enough to be picked up by the Romanian authorities were returned to the Bulgarian authorities where they were imprisoned for attempting to leave the country without official permission under Article 279 of the Bulgarian Criminal Code. There have been unconfirmed reports that some were also returned by the Greek authorities before they could register as political refugees and have their cases examined, although in most cases such refugees were granted asylum by the Greek authorities. Those who fled to Yugoslavia were held for up to 14 days (as is Yugoslav practice) and then allowed to travel to Turkey without hindrance. Refugees report that the Yugoslav authorities treated them well and were sympathetic to their plight.

Continued resistance

Although the largest incidents of active resistance to the assimilation policy occurred in the initial period of December 1984 to March 1985 and mostly in the south of the country, resistance continued. For example four people from Drandar near Varna were among the leaders of a group that produced thousands of leaflets which were distributed in early June 1986 to ethnic Turkish villages in the environs of Varna, Tolbuhin and Silistra. These leaflets called on ethnic Turks to show their opposition to the assimilation campaign by boycotting the forthcoming elections to the National Assembly. They, along with the other leaders, were arrested and tried *in camera* and sentenced to between eight and ten years' imprisonment. A number of other ethnic Turks involved in the actual distribution of the leaflets were also arrested and received milder sentences. The Bulgarian authorities have stated that the four men were convicted for belonging to a group with terrorist aims although the available information appears to contradict this charge.

Ethnic Turks have however on occasion resorted to terrorism, apparently in protest at the assimilation campaign. On 8 July 1987 three men were killed in a shoot-out with anti-terrorist forces at a main tourist hotel in Varna during a siege after the men had taken schoolchildren as hostages. BTA on 9 July 1987 released only a minimum of information and gave the names of the dead men as N. Nikolov, O. Nikolov and N. Asenov. However emigre sources state that this official unwillingness to disclose detailed information was because the three men were ethnic Turks from Dulovo in Silistra District who were attempting to escape from Bulgaria. Other emigre sources in Turkey state that two of the men were named Apti and Orhan Nedzhibov (father and son presumably renamed Nikolov in the campaign) and again stated that all three were ethnic Turks protesting against the assimilation campaign.

Another case predates the name-changing campaign. On 25 April 1988 three men were sentenced to death and four others, including a woman, received sentences of between one and five years for being responsible for a series of bomb attacks in which eight people died including two children and

51 were injured. The attacks began on 30 August 1984 with an explosion in the waiting room of Plovdiv railway station and one at Varna airport. Other explosions occurred on a passenger train and at a hotel in Sliven. The last attack was on 9 March 1985. BTA in late April 1988 gave the names of the three men as Elin Madzharov, Altsek Chakurov and Sava Georgiev. Emigre sources in Turkey confirmed that these three men were ethnic Turks previously named Emin Aliev, Abdullah Chakirov and Safet Guney respectively and claim that their motives were to protest against the assimilation campaign. Again, lack of detailed information makes this hard to verify but the inclusion of their names by the Bulgarian Deputy Foreign Minister Ivan Ganev (in a statement of 15 June 1989 to the Ambassadors of countries participating in the CSCE process at a conference in Paris) in a list of people alleged to have been operating under orders of the Turkish secret service would appear to confirm this.

When the explosions began they were welcomed by some Slav Bulgarian emigre circles hostile to the present regime in Bulgaria like those in Paris centred around the journal *Badeshte* (*The Future*) who implicitly claimed the actions as part of the Bulgarian Liberation Movement which they support. The appearance of leaflets stating '40 Years: 40 Bombs' after the August 1984 explosions perhaps shows that the outrages were more anti-communist than anti-assimilation — Bulgaria was just preparing to celebrate 40 years since the communist take-over of power in September 1944. *Badeshte* and the Bulgarian Liberation Movement have been active in joining Turkish protests at the assimilation campaign. However, this has not been true of all such emigre groups. For example a group in West Germany has publicly applauded the assimilation campaign despite their antagonism to the present Bulgarian authorities — demonstrating again the depth of national feeling held by some Bulgarians against Turks.

Official information and disinformation

The Bulgarian authorities made no official statements about the name-changing campaign until reports began to appear in the foreign press in early 1985. Since then the authorities have consistently denied both the existence of an ethnic Turkish minority in Bulgaria and that the name-changing was anything other than voluntary and spontaneous. To support their claim to the non-existence of the minority the Bulgarian authorities have used carefully selected historical sources, especially an article by Midhat Pasha, the Grand Vizier of the Ottoman Empire, published in a French journal in 1878. This article states:

'Firstly, it must be borne in mind that among the Bulgarians who arouse so much interest there are more than one million Moslems. These Moslems did not come from Asia to establish themselves in Bulgaria, as is widely believed. They are themselves descendants of those Bulgarians converted to Islam at the time of the conquest and during the following years. They are children of one common country, from one common race, and share a common origin.'[30]

The Bulgarian authorities however ignore the many contradictory historical sources and since the name-changing campaign began historians within Bulgaria are obliged to reflect the new policy. This has been to the advantage of Professor Petar Petrov, a renowned anti-Turk whose work has played an important part in current official propaganda while his opponents within Bulgaria have been denied publication, for example Strashimir Dimitrov whose book on the Turkish colonization was stopped in 1985.[31]

Another facet of the new policy is illustrated by the report in the official Bulgarian daily *Otechestven Front* in January 1986 which summarized the purported 'discoveries' of 30 years of studies by Bulgarian research anthropologists. Apparently experts of the Bulgarian Academy of Science's Institute of Morphology carried out 'intensive research' in the districts of Blagoevgrad, Smolyan and Kardzhali on over 6000 men and women which showed, reported *Otechestven Front*, that all the inhabitants proved to be Bulgarians, Bulgarian-Moslems and descendants of a section of the Bulgarian population subjected to ethnic assimilation (by the Turks).[32]

Such 'research', apparently utilizing such methods as skull-measurements, is reminiscent of Nazi Germany and has had little impact on outside opinion. More successful has been the Bulgarian authorities attempts to discredit accusations, many of which inevitably have originated from Turkey, by pointing to Turkey's own massive human rights violations and lamentable record regarding her own minorities like the Kurds. The Bulgarian authorities have also claimed that reports alleging a forced assimilation campaign are part of a concerted attempt to discredit socialist Bulgaria — an attempt which includes allegations of Bulgarian complicity in the attempted assassination of Pope John Paul II and gun and drug trafficking.[33]

Additionally, beginning in April 1986 there have been a number of statements in the official media rigorously denying all allegations of human rights abuses or that the name-changing was other than 'a benevolent, spontaneous and sincere process by persons who have taken cognizance of their Bulgarian origins' (BTA 2 April 1986). However such statements have at times contradicted each other. For example, in one statement, purported victims apparently did not exist and had never existed in Bulgaria after the authorities had apparently checked with the aid of the 'computers of the unified system of public records registration and administrative service (ESGRAON)' while in other publications the same people were reported to be alive and well in the villages where they were known to have originated. In other instances letters signed under duress have been published to counter human rights allegations as part of an official policy of disinformation. One example among many concerns the killing by security forces of Ayshe Myumyunova and her brother's child during the demonstration in December 1984 in Benkovski.[34] The Bulgarian authorities have resolutely denied such killings and have produced death certificates and declarations to back up their claims that both Ayshe Myumyunova and Fatmen Yun's child died of natural causes — the Bulgarian authorities apparently knew which child was alleged to have died without even knowing the name as eyewitnesses only knew the first name of the mother. However a variety of eyewitnesses testified to the contrary and one, who was expelled from Bulgaria on 19 May 1989, stated that Ayshe Myunyunova was shot in the heart while the child was shot in the head. He further stated that the grandfather was forced to sign a declaration that the child had died of natural causes and a doctor, Fikret Eyyubov, was pressured to sign a false death certificate but refused and as a result was sent to Belene camp for one year followed by internment in Bobovdol prison camp. It appears that other doctors had less qualms or were more susceptible to official pressure. Another refugee testified that he saw, on 7 March 1987 while he was employed at Kardzhali Hospital, officials in the morgue of the hospital burning documents relating to the deaths of ethnic Turks.

Despite these denials, statements made by leading Bulgarian officials implicitly acknowledge that the name-changing campaign has met with resistance. For example Stoyan Stoyanov, First Secretary of the Haskovo District Party Committee, stated in a speech in mid-1985 that some ethnic Turks 'had not yet matured sufficiently politically to accept new names' and that there had been 'sporadic instances of anti-social meetings' and of people 'favouring outdated traditions such as religious burials, circumcision and attendance at mosques'.[35] Other leading officials have made statements referring to forced internal resettlement of objectors and penalties for circumcision and a number of official documents have come to light which confirm reported aspects of the assimilation campaign.

The events of May 1989

The situation of small-scale sporadic protest arising out of a largely passive albeit sullen acceptance of the status quo by the ethnic Turkish population radically changed in early 1989 with the mass participation in various unofficial protest groups and large-scale protest action on a country-wide basis. The Bulgaria authorities responded with violent repression and mass expulsions of thousands of activists. This in turn was followed by a general exodus of ethnic Turks taking advantage of the previously unavailable opportunities of leaving Bulgaria for a new life in Turkey. In late June 1989 the number of refugees exceeded 60,000 with thousands more leaving each day and no sign of the flood abating. Official Bulgarian statements stated that 150,000 passports had been issued and another 100,000 applications received.[36] By late August over 300,000 had left for Turkey.

The formation of opposition groups

On 16 January 1988 six Bulgarian dissidents set up an **Independent Association for the Defence of Human Rights in Bulgaria** (IADHR) and, despite severe harassment by the authorities with many founder members forced into internal exile or emigration, the association has continued to function and from the outset has taken up the issue of the repression against the ethnic Turks — this in marked contrast to a group ostensibly with similar aims set up with official backing as a rival in June 1988 under the chairmanship of Konstantin Tellalov, a former ambassador to the UN and a significant figure in the Bulgarian power hierarchy, now retired. This latter group is seen by all Bulgarian dissidents from every ethnic group as merely a government front organization.

The IADHR soon attracted Turkish members, such as 29-year-old Zeynep Ibrahimova from Kliment village in Shumen district who had refused to use her new Bulgarian name and who had served 17 months of a two-year prison sentence imposed on 23 August 1985 after attempting to flee to Turkey. Following her release from Sliven Prison for Women, she was interned in Botevo in Mihailvgrad district for two years along with her brother, Ibrahim Ibrahimov, who had been tried and sentenced with her for attempting to flee the country. They and two others were the first Turks to join IADHR in October 1988. She was elected the association's representative in the Varna region. On 31 January 1989 the association issued a list of 36 new active members willing to be publicly identified, 23 of whom were ethnic Turks using their illegal Turkish/Arabic names. When Zeynep Ibrahimova was expelled from Bulgaria on 3 February 1989 there were about 50 Turks in the IADHR out of a total of some 350 but by June the number of Turks exceeded that of Bulgarians due to their radicalization in May and June 1989.

Furthermore a specifically Turkish civil rights group within Bulgaria was formed in late 1988, called the **Democratic League for the Defence of the Rights of Man** with the aim of, among other things, opposing the assimilation campaign and the repression of Islam. The chairman, Mustafa Yumerov, a philosopher, was internally exiled in Komarevo village near Vratsa, while the two secretaries, Sabri Iskenderov and Ali Ormanliev, were also subject to internal exile in Kameno Pole and Drashak respectively — villages in Vratsa region — both men having served sentences in Belene prison camp in connection with the assimilation campaign. The Democratic League quickly attracted a very large membership and applied without success for legal recognition and sent an open letter containing its aims to Todor Zhivkov.

In addition on 30 January 1989 a third association — **The Association for the Support of Vienna 1989** (ASV89) was set up in the village of Zornitsa in Haskovo region under the leadership of Avni Veliev — a former political prisoner sentenced in Kardzhali on 5 February 1985 to seven years 10 months' imprisonment for anti-state activities under Articles 108 and 109 of the criminal code and who had just been released from prison on 29 December 1988. This organization's name was due to the attempt to bring to the attention of the world public the plight of ethnic Turks in Bulgaria at the time of the CSCE Conference on Human Rights in Paris in early June 1989.

These three independent organizations (IADHR, The Democratic League, and ASV89) all had good connections with each other and quickly attracted thousands of professed members. The two primary Turkish organizations, the Democratic League and ASV89, in particular were able to spread throughout the country mainly in the predominately Turkish inhabited areas but also in other areas where there were large numbers of activist Turks in forced exile. An essential factor in their dramatic growth in support and the country-wide action they were able to undertake was the small amount of leeway afforded them due to the international climate of 'Glasnost' on the part of the USSR and the corresponding slight easing within Bulgaria — especially and vitally in the field of radio communications. Due to this changed international climate the Bulgarian authorities stopped jamming the BBC, Deutsche Welle, and Radio Free Europe (RFE) — although RFE occasionally was still jammed as was Turkish Radio. This, combined with the easing of telephone links with the west, allowed the new organizations to use foreign radio stations as essential means of communication which previously had been denied them. The growth of support for ASV89 is an excellent example of this. After Avni Veliev set up ASV89 in January, with Ismet Emrullov Ismailov from Dzhebel as secretary, he managed to contact RFE on 2 May by telephone and informed them of the programme and aims of the organization. Between 5 and 11 May RFE repeatedly broadcasted his message and as a result many ethnic Turks from all over the country got to hear about it. Some made cassettes of the RFE report and these were distributed as far north as Shumen attracting support.

Mass protest — hunger strikes, demonstrations and violent repression

Hunger strikes had been used by many ethnic Turks in Belene and elsewhere as a means of protest against the assimilation campaign and the ensuing arrests, or in attempts to get permission to emigrate, but it was the publicizing of such actions within Bulgaria by foreign radio stations which was the crucial difference in 1989. The breaking of the authorities' monopoly on information within the country allowed the new organizations to coordinate mass protest which began again in May 1989 with hunger strikes by ethnic Turks in Silistra, Shumen and Razgrad and some other villages in the north east.

The numbers on hunger strike rose from 30 to approximately 200 by mid-May[37] to over 1000 by mid-June and there were corresponding peaceful demonstrations in support by hundreds of ethnic Turks, mostly women and children, in Silistra and Shumen on 14/ 15 May. More hunger strikers publicized their actions via foreign radio stations and mass demonstrations occurred in late May throughout the north-east (Kaolinovo, Ezerche, Razgrad, Todor Ikonomovo, Tolbuhin) and in the south (Dzhebel) of the country where ethnic Turks predominate. The authorities responded with force and many (reportedly the number was as high as 60)[38] demonstrators were killed. Most deaths were from gunshot wounds after troops opened fire on protesting crowds or some from injuries received from beatings.

For example on 24 May a demonstration of about 1000 people including women and children took place in Ezerche near Razgrad in the north-east at 10 p.m. According to eyewitness accounts, the local Communist Party secretary met the crowd and asked for their demands, and the crowd replied that they wanted their old names back etc. Three lorries arrived with troops and despite the fact that all accounts state that the demonstration was peaceful the troops opened fire after orders from a Bulgarian official named Markov and two demonstrators were shot dead: Ahmet Burukov, aged 38, shot in the forehead and back of the head; and Sezgin Saliev Karaomerov aged 18, shot in the heart. Another example is a demonstration in Kaolinovo on 20 May which was the climax of a protest march which had begun in Pristoe and continued through the neighbouring villages of Kliment, Naum and Takach before arriving in Kaolinovo several thousand strong. Again eyewitnesses state that the troops opened fire without provocation and one eyewitness saw Nedzheb Osmanov Nedzhebov, a 47-year-old bus driver from Kus, clubbed to the ground by blows from a rifle butt and killed. The official cause of his death was reported to be heart failure.

Other deaths have been reported following beatings which were widespread and indiscriminate throughout all ethnic Turkish regions in the north-east and south. Following the mass demonstrations involving thousands of participants, most affected areas were quickly put under martial law with troops and tanks and fire-engines (water-canon was widely used as crowd control) installed. In the southern regions, especially in Dzhebel, the authorities began widespread beatings, going from house to house and indiscriminately beating the inhabitants. Similarly those caught in the streets faced arbitrary beatings and for three days, beginning on 22 May — 'Bloody Monday' — nobody in the city of Dzhebel was allowed to leave their house.

On 23 May 1989 BTA issued a statement admitting that demonstrations had occurred but claimed that they were caused by misapprehension about the soon to be introduced new passport law, and incitement from foreign radio stations and extremists. BTA admitted that three people had died but stated that one had died from heart failure while the other two had died from ricocheting bullets fired as warning shots. On 15 June in a statement to the Ambassadors of countries participating in the CSCE process at the conference held in Paris, Deputy Foreign Minister Ivan Ganev gave a detailed list of demonstrations and 'disorders' which had taken place in Bulgaria between 20 and 27 May which had resulted in, he said, seven deaths and 28 people wounded. He said that demonstrations had taken place in Kaolinovo, Todor Ikonomovo, Razgrad, Dulovo, Vokil, Oven, Poroyno, Cherkovna, Vodno, Isperich, Dzhebel, Ezerche, Dulgopol, Beli Lom, Omurtag, Shumen, Medovets, Gradnitsa and Benkovski. However he denied that the demonstrations were peaceful, alleging that in cases rioters had set fire to houses of 'Bulgarian Muslims' (i.e. ethnic Turks) who did not want to emigrate and had vandalized cars and shop windows, and stated that the authorities had been obliged to resort to force to restore public order. He also denied that anybody had been expelled from Bulgaria and extensively blamed the activities of the Turkish secret services in fomenting trouble among ethnic Turks. On 1 June the Bulgarian authorities organized their own official demonstrations in Shumen,

Pleven, Razgrad, Targovishte, Kubrat, Popovo, and Burgas against 'Turkish interference' in Bulgaria.[39]

Mass expulsions

In tandem with the policy of attempted intimidation through force, the authorities embarked on a policy of expelling activists from Bulgaria. All the initial Turkish leaders of the three organizations (IADHR, the Democratic League and ASV89) were expelled by the end of May and the expulsions soon grew into a flood. Some 500 had been expelled by 7 June but the number had risen to 14,000 by 14 June according to Turkish television and there were thousands arriving each day. By late June the figure had reached 60,000 with reports of 250,000 more to come.[40] The sheer size of the numbers involved indicate that while the first to be expelled were activists, many of whom did not want to leave but left due to the threat of imprisonment or other threats to them or their families, the authorities apparently seem to be allowing large numbers to emigrate. Many ethnic Turks have decided that the policy of forced assimilation and the attendant official repression is such that there is no future for them in Bulgaria and despite having to give up, in many cases, a settled life of financial security have opted for a new life in Turkey. Many, especially those expelled in or before May were given only a few hours notice and were not allowed to take more than a small bag and no money. All were obliged to leave houses and other valuables behind and some were informed by the authorities that if they returned within five years they could reclaim their property. Again, the more recent refugees have been able to leave with, in some cases, more possessions (cars, water heaters etc. and a limited amount of money) although the valuables left behind remain considerable.

Whether the Bulgarian authorities have decided to solve the problem of the Turkish minority by expelling the bulk of them remains to be seen. The Bulgarian government has officially recognized the economic problems incurred by the refugees as most of those leaving were highly skilled farmers who, with Bulgaria's labour shortage, will be difficult to replace. Ivan Angelov, a senior advisor to the Council of Ministers, told a press conference in Sofia that a decree had been passed introducing longer working hours and moving workers into the affected areas. In addition he stated that the refugees had removed huge amounts of savings from Bulgarian banks which may cause severe financial problems for Bulgaria.[41]

Refugees

Virtually all of the large number of refugees have come to Turkey where many have relatives due to the previous waves of emigration. In the beginning those expelled were often given passports with visas not for Turkey but for other non-Comecon countries like Austria, Yugoslavia or even Sweden and were obliged to pay the authorities for their train tickets out of the country and then had to find their way to Turkey. Some, from the north-east, were even expelled to Romania and then had to make their way to Vienna. However by early June the bulk of refugees were arriving directly in Turkey.

The arrival of such large numbers of refugees, often with only minimal financial means, has been problematic for the Turkish authorities. However, the Turkish government has proved to be extremely sympathetic to the plight of the Bulgarian Turks. On 7 June 1989 television announced that the government had passed a decree which would allow the refugees to be immediately accepted as Turkish citizens without the previous waiting period of two years and on 11 June it was announced that the Bulgarian currency, the leva, could be changed at Turkish banks. At a meeting of emigre associations on 7 June the mayor of Bakirkoy — one of

Istanbul's largest districts — promised substantial material help for the refugees in the shape of employment and housing, and the government has helped to establish 'tent cities' (like that in Kirklarele near Edirne at the border with Bulgaria, which was announced on Turkish television on 10 June 1989) for those temporarily without accommodation. Similarly the emigre associations have been working around the clock to try and cope with the huge flood of refugees. Additionally the Turkish government announced that it would raise the question of possessions and property which the refugees have been forced to leave behind in Bulgaria.[42]

Over 300,000 had arrived by late August and there were reports of Bulgarian troops entering villages, especially Pomak villages, to prevent the exodus. At the same time Turkey closed the border and reimposed visa restrictions on citizens from Bugaria. By mid-September over 13,000 had returned to Bulgaria probably due to the economic uncertainty facing them in Turkey although Turkish officials claim that most of those returning have done so due to fears of reprisals against remaining relatives in Bulgaria. Turkey has also charged that some of those who returned have been denied access to their old homes and sent to labour camps.

Support for ethnic Turks by Bulgarians

The alliance between ethnic Turks and Bulgarians shown in the membership of the IADHR has been mirrored by the presence of Bulgarians participating with ethnic Turks in some of the demonstrations, such as that of 27 May in Targovishte when about 100 Bulgarians joined the demonstration. In addition there have been a number of declarations by Bulgarians deploring the use of violence by the authorities against ethnic Turkish demonstrators and calling for an end to the assimilation policy, e.g. that of 22 May by the national leadership of the IADHR and again on 23/24 May by Anton Zapryanov of the IADHR and Father Hristofor Sabev of another newly formed independent group — **The Committee for Religious Rights**.[43] This latter group was set up by provincial Orthodox priests; Sabev is from Veliko Tarnovo, and calls for religious freedom for Muslims as well as greater freedom for Christians of all denominations. Amnesty International reported that Anton Zapryanov and Konstantin Trenchev, president of an underground trade union movement set up in February 1989, were arrested in late May apparently on charges of having fermented the wave of unrest amongst the ethnic Turks.[44]

Many ethnic Turk refugees state that they encountered little animosity from ordinary Bulgarians but reported that many Bulgarians living in regions predominately inhabited by Turks, especially in the south around Kardzhali, viewed the mass demonstrations with considerable unease due to government propaganda which implied that the Turks would attack them. However all the protests have been directed at government policy and there have been no reports of such inter-ethnic violence.

The international response

Bulgaria is a small country widely viewed as one of the USSR's most loyal allies. As such it enjoys less world press coverage than, for example, Poland. The assimilation campaign has been widely reported but the difficulties in obtaining information prior to the events of May 1989 — due to extreme official censorship — have made such reporting problematic. Inevitably, perhaps, the Turkish government has been the main foreign power to raise the issue at international forums but Turkey's treatment of its own minorities, such as the Kurds, and its record on human rights abuses have allowed the Bulgarian government to deflect criticism; statements made by Turgut Ozal, the Turkish Prime Minister at an election rally in Bursa, threatening action against Bulgaria similar to that taken by Turkey in Cyprus have not helped.

However various human rights groups have repeatedly raised the issue both with the Bulgarian government and in the UN. Amnesty International twice, in June 1986 and May 1987, submitted its concerns in Bulgaria to the UN under the procedure for confidentially reviewing communications about human rights abuses (the so-called '1503 procedure') and the organization visited Bulgaria and met with officials to discuss these concerns. The Bulgarian government made available a large amount of information on individual cases but Amnesty International remained concerned and has pointed out the unreliability of some of the information received from official Bulgarian sources.[45] It can hardly be coincidence that Bulgaria is some five years overdue, despite repeated reminders by the UN, in her second periodic report to the Human Rights Committee of the UN on Bulgaria's compliance with the terms of the International Covenant on Civil and Political Rights which she ratified on 21 September 1970.

Western governments have also raised the issue on many occasions, but not with the vehemence that others — like Turkey — would prefer although the events of May and the expulsions have prompted greater censure. On 13 June the US State Department refused to meet Konstantin Glavanakov, Deputy Minister for Foreign Trade, due to 'Bulgaria's violent actions against its ethnic Turkish minority', and Western diplomats at the Paris CSCE conference were reported as trying to persuade Bulgaria to accept neutral mediation, either by Austria or Switzerland, on the ethnic Turkish issue but the Bulgarian delegation adamantly refused.[46] Various Islamic countries have condemned Bulgaria and the OIC sent a delegation to Bulgaria which reported on religious restrictions for Muslims. However some Arab countries like Syria which are more closely allied to Bulgaria have supported Bulgaria in the international propaganda arena. It has also been noticeable that there has been little support for Bulgaria from her erstwhile allies in Comecon on this issue, and the one-day visit by Todor Zhivkov to Moscow fuelled speculation about Soviet unease at Bulgaria's assimilation policies.[47]

The Socialist Republic of Macedonia (Yugoslavia)

The Macedonians

Macedonia — the geographical area bounded to the north by the Skopska Crna Gora and the Shar Planina mountains; to the east by the Rila and Rhodope mountains; to the south by the Aegean coast around Salonika, Mount Olympus and the Pindus mountains; and to the west by the lakes of Ohrid and Prespa; and comprising approximately 67,000 sq.kms. — is currently divided between Yugoslavia, Greece and Bulgaria. Macedonia was one of the first areas in the Balkan peninsula to be conquered by the Ottoman empire and was one of the last to be liberated during the Balkan Wars of 1912/13.

History

As noted above, the founding of the Exarchate church in 1870 had pitted Greek against Bulgarian in Macedonia and the aborted 'Greater Bulgaria' of the San Stefano treaty, annulled by the Treaty of Berlin, made the new Bulgarian state permanently revisionist and revanchist. Another aspect of the Treaty of Berlin was the administration of Bosnia-Herzegovina and the garrisoning of the Sanjak of Novibazar, dividing Serbia and Montenegro, by Austro-Hungary, resulting in Serbia also looking towards Macedonia for future expansion as her 'natural' territories for expansion (i.e. those territories with large Serbian populations) fell under Austro-Hungarian control. After defeat by Bulgaria in 1885 Serbia actively pursued an expansionist policy in Macedonia, calling it South Serbia and claiming that Slav Macedonians were Serbs. The Society of Saint Sava was founded in 1886 to promote Serbian nationalism, especially in Macedonia. By the mid-1890s Serbia claimed 100 Serbian schools in Macedonia to the Bulgarian's 600-700 schools, mostly under the aegis of the Exarchate church. The Greeks also founded a society similar to the Serbs, the *Ethnike Hetairia*, which aimed to liberate all Greeks still within the Ottoman Empire beginning with those in Macedonia including the Slav-speaking population who they called Slavophone Greeks. This society was supported by three-quarters of Greek army officers and had many wealthy patrons. By 1895 the Greeks claimed 1400 schools in Macedonia and were spending proportionately more on education in Macedonia, which was still within the Ottoman Empire, than in Greece itself. The Vlachs scattered in Western Macedonia, Epirus and Thessaly, who speak a form of Romanian, allowed the Romanians also to make a claim and by 1912 they also were subsidising over 30 schools.

Within Macedonia itself the Internal Macedonian Revolutionary Organization (IMRO) was set up in 1893 and was against partition of Macedonia and supported the idea of a south Slav federation of Serbs, Macedonians and Bulgarians. This organization won wide support and made plans for an armed uprising. However huge numbers of Macedonians had fled to Bulgaria following the failure of the San Stefano 'Greater Bulgaria' — by 1903 almost half the population of Sofia was comprised of Macedonian refugees or immigrants — and this mass of refugees, as well as destabilising Bulgaria internally for many years, allowed a rival organization to IMRO, the External Organization or Supremacists, to be set up in Sofia in 1895 which aimed at the incorporation of Macedonia within Bulgaria, i.e. the 'Greater Bulgaria'. Thus almost from the outset IMRO was fatally divided in its aims between those who wanted Macedonia for Bulgaria and those who wanted a separate Macedonian state either within some form of federation or independent.

The overall result of all these competing rivalries in Macedonia was disastrous for the actual population, which by most accounts was sympathetic to one of the wings of IMRO, with the peasants being subjected to repeated visits by armed gangs from the IMRO factions, Serbs, Bulgarians and Greeks as well as the Ottoman authorities until the Balkan Wars when the Ottoman empire was finally driven out of Macedonia.

Since then the portion now in Yugoslavia — Vardar Macedonia — has, except during the two world wars when for a sizeable period most of it was occupied by Bulgaria — belonged firstly to Serbia and then to the Kingdom of Serbs, Croats and Slovenes, later known as Yugoslavia, which came into existence in December 1918. In line with Serbian claims that the Macedonians were in fact Southern Serbs, the church was put under the control of the Serbian Patriarchate and Serbian, the official language, became compulsory both in schools and public life. This policy alienated the population and spread pro-Bulgarian feeling.

During World War II, Bulgaria, allied to Nazi Germany, occupied most of Vardar Macedonia, and although Hitler did not allow Bulgaria to formally annex the territories they occupied both in Yugoslavia and Greece, the Bulgarian government acted as if they had. Bulgarian officials were sent in, teachers were replaced by Bulgarian ones, and the July 1942 law on citizenship resulted in the exodus of many Serbs to Serbia. However, despite being welcomed by many as liberators, the attitude of the Bulgarians (the Ministry of the Interior even had to warn that officials who treated Macedonia as a foreign country would be punished) quickly led to disillusionment by the population of Vardar Macedonia. Pro-Bulgarian sentiment meant that the Partisans, the Yugoslav communist resistance movement led by Tito, had initially made little headway in Macedonia but this situation changed after the visit to Skopje of Tito's aide Vukmanovic-Tempo and by the end of 1943 the Partisans were becoming increasingly popular, resulting in Bulgarian reprisals which further alienated the population. In 1944 Bulgarian troops began to desert to the Partisans and in September 1944 Bulgaria changed sides and joined the allies. The Bulgarian occupation of 1941-44 had disillusioned many, if not most, Yugoslav Macedonians but there remained a residual pro-Bulgarian sentiment.

The Yugoslav Communist Party's attitude to the Macedonian question underwent successive changes. Up till 1934/5 the Comintern, the international communist movement orchestrated from Moscow, was revisionist regarding the boundaries of Yugoslavia and called for a united Macedonia similar to that of one of the factions of IMRO. In line with this, a 'United IMRO' was set up under communist aegis but this new organization did not prove a great success. Hitler's rise to power, with the result that Germany now became the leading revisionist power in Europe, heralded a change in the Comintern line to that of the Popular Fronts. During World War II, under Tito's leadership, the Partisans resolved to create a Macedonian republic within a new federal Yugoslavia. This republic was seen as providing a bridge between Yugoslavia and Bulgaria which would be united in a Balkan federation which might also include Albania which was also under communist control after the war, and Greece where there was a civil war between the communists and non-communists for control. The Bulgarian leader, Georgi Dimitrov, both of whose parents were from Macedonia, was receptive to Tito's plans of uniting Vardar Macedonia in Yugoslavia with Pirin Macedonia in Bulgaria, but his death in July 1949 and the break between Tito and Stalin over Tito's ambitions made the Yugoslav-Bulgarian cooperation a short-lived affair. Henceforth relations between the new Macedonian republic and Bulgaria would be strained and this situation has lasted till the present.

In Vardar Macedonia the new authorities quickly set about consolidating their position. The new nation needed a written language and, initially, the spoken dialect of northern Macedonia was chosen as the basis for the Macedonian language, but this was deemed as too close to Serbian and the dialects of Bitola-Veles became the norm.[48] These dialects were closer to the Bulgarian literary language but as the Bulgarian was based upon the eastern Bulgarian dialects it allowed enough differentiation for the Yugoslavs to claim that it was a language distinct from Bulgarian — a point which Bulgaria has bitterly disputed ever since.[49] In fact, the differentiation between the Macedonian dialects and the Bulgarian ones becomes progressively less pronounced on an east-west basis. Whether Macedonian, which shares nearly all the same distinct characteristics which separate Bulgarian from other Slav languages — lack of cases; the post-positive definitive article; the replacement of the infinitive form; and the preservation of the simple verbal forms for the past and imperfect tenses — is truly a different language from Bulgarian or merely a dialect of it, is a moot point. The alphabet was accepted on 3 May 1945, the orthography on 7 June 1945 and the first primer in the new language appeared by 1946 which year also saw the founding of a Macedonian Department of the Faculty of Philosophy in Skopje. A grammar of the Macedonian Literary Language appeared in 1952, and the Institute for the Macedonian Language 'Krste P. Misirkov' was founded in 1953. Since World War II the new republic has used the full weight of the education system and the bureaucracy to make the new language common parlance, indeed it is noticeable still that old people tend to speak a mixture of dialects which include obvious Serbianisms and Bulgarianisms while those young enough to have gone through the educational system in its entirety speak a 'purer' Macedonian.

In addition to the new language the new republic needed a history and the new school textbooks quickly reflected this need by tracing the Macedonian nation back through history. Again this has caused bitter resentment from Bulgaria as the Macedonian historical figures are also claimed by Bulgaria as Bulgarian heroes, e.g. Gotse Delchev who was one of the leaders of, and died in, the abortive rising of 1903 in Macedonia — Macedonian textbooks even hint at Bulgarian complicity in his death at the hands of the Ottomans[50] — and the medieval emperor Samuil whose empire was centred around lake Ohrid.

Religion

Religion was another important tool for the new authorities and the freeing of the Orthodox church in Yugoslav Macedonia from Serbian control with the autocephalous Macedonian Orthodox Church and the revival of the ancient archbishopric of Ohrid in 1958 was an important step along the path to nationhood — a rare occurrence of atheist state cooperation with organized religion. This move was resisted by the Serbian Orthodox Church as was the final declaration of the autocephalous status of the Macedonian Church on 18 July 1967. The Serbian Orthodox Church, along with the other Orthodox churches, remains firm in its refusal to recognize the Macedonian Church. Relations between the Macedonian Orthodox Church and the authorities in Yugoslav Macedonia have continued to be good, aided by a common front against the threat of Albanian nationalism and the attendant growth of Islam.

Official unease

Thus the new authorities overcame the residual pro-Bulgarian feeling among much of the population and the split

with Bulgaria in 1948 and apparently have been successful in building a distinct national consciousness based on the available differences between Macedonia and Bulgaria proper. The change from the pre-war situation of unrecognized minority status and attempted assimilation by Serbia to the current one where the Macedonians are the majority people in their own republic with considerable autonomy within Yugoslavia's federation/confederation has obvious attractions. The authorities have also been aided by the comparative lack of attraction for its population of Bulgaria, which remained within the Soviet bloc, in comparison to the new Yugoslavia. However the current desperate economic, political and social situation in Yugoslavia and the national question of the Albanians within Yugoslavia which threatens the republic probably more than any of the other republics including Serbia, as well as Bulgaria's continuing ambitions make the future still problematic for the Macedonian republic.

An additional factor maybe the resurgence of Serbian nationalism which may once more reclaim Macedonia as 'Southern Serbia', although there is little sign of this at present. The unease of the current authorities is shown by the never-ending polemics with Bulgaria, the treatment of Albanian nationalism, and the harsh attitude to emigre groups deemed hostile to the republic. An example of this is the 13-year prison sentence imposed by Skopje district court in 1979 on Dragan Bogdanovski, a Macedonian emigre, for leading an organization calling for a united independent Macedonian state which would incorporate not only the Yugoslav republic of Macedonia but also the Macedonian territories in Greece and Bulgaria — ironically a similar aim to that of Gotse Delchev who is lionized by the authorities.[51]

The population of the Socialist Republic of Macedonia was 1,912,257 as measured by the census of 1981, of which there were 1,281,195 Macedonians, 377,726 Albanians, 44,613 Serbs, 39,555 Moslems, 47,223 Gypsies, 86,691 Turks and 7,190 Vlachs, the remainder consisting of a variety of other ethnic groups. There were also 1,984 Bulgarians (as opposed to Macedonians) recorded.

The Albanians

The ethnic Albanians, by far the largest minority in the Socialist Republic of Macedonia, live in compact settlements in the west of the republic bordering on Albania, the north-west bordering on the predominately Albanian province of Kosovo and in Skopje where they make up over 14% of the population and in Kumanovo where they are about one third of the population. They constitute a majority of the population in many western areas, notably the districts of: Tetovo — about 113,000 Albanians to 38,000 Macedonians; Gostivar — 63,000 to 18,000; Kicevo — 23,000 to 21,000; and Debar — 10,000 to 2500. In the towns the difference is not so marked; for example, there are some 22,000 Albanians, 18,000 Macedonians and 2000 Turks in Tetovo itself.[52]

Population growth

There were 377,726 Albanians as per the census of 1981, comprising 19.8% of the population which shows an increase of slightly more than 36% over the figures in the previous census of 1971 when there were 279,871 Albanians (17% of the population). Thus the Albanians have a considerably higher birth rate than the Macedonians and a delegate from Tetovo reported to the Macedonian League of Communists on 26 April 1988 that the birth rate in Tetovo, an area of high Albanian concentration, was three times the national average. The situation regarding the position of the Albanians vis-à-vis the Macedonians is reminiscent of that of the ethnic Turks vis-à-vis the Bulgarians in Bulgaria — a sizeable minority with a far higher growth rate, speaking a different language, living in concentrated areas especially in the countryside, and whose geographical position gives rise to a possible irredenta.

Education and culture

Yugoslavia is Europe's multi-national state par excellence and the inter-war period was bedevilled by rivalries between the different nationalities, especially the Serbs and Croats, and ethnic groups. The post-war Yugoslav authorities pledged to solve the country's seemingly intractable national problems under the slogan of 'Brotherhood and Unity' and, as noted above, the Macedonians were recognized for the first time as a separate nation. The Albanians are recognized as a nationality of Yugoslavia, not as a nation as the Albanian national 'home' is outside of Yugoslavia, and as such have a number of education and cultural rights. By 1951 there were over 200 Albanian schools in Macedonia employing over 600 teachers and catering for over 26,000 pupils, and by 1973 this had been expanded to 248 schools employing 2150 teachers and over 60,000 pupils.[53] In 1981 Tanjug, the official Yugoslav news agency, reported on 9 July that there were 287 Albanian language elementary schools employing about 3000 teachers with over 74,000 pupils in Macedonia with a further 8200 in secondary schools attending classes in the Albanian language — figures which have changed little according to the Bosnian newspaper *Oslobodjenje* of 6 January 1989. There were also, in 1980, 2365 students of Albanian nationality enrolled at university-level institutions. Additionally there is an Albanian newspaper *Flaka e Vellazerimit*, Albanian television and radio programmes, and many Albanian cultural associations, theatre groups, sports clubs, etc.

However in reality the picture is not as harmonious as the above indicates.

The growth of Albanian nationalism and the authorities' reaction

The majority of Yugoslavia's Albanian population lives in the neighbouring province of Kosovo where they constitute a large majority of the population. This province is part of the republic of Serbia and is seen by the Serbs as the cradle of Serbian nationhood. Relations between Albanians and Serbs in Kosovo have traditionally been tense and this was exacerbated after the war by the attitude of the powerful Alexander Rankovic, a Serb who was head of the feared security apparatus. Yugoslavia means the 'land of the south Slavs' and the Albanians are not Slavs and did not feel themselves to be particularly a part of the new state. In the republic of Macedonia all the ethnic minorities with the exception of the Serbs have a smaller proportion of membership in the League of Communists (LC) than their porportion in the population. For example the membership of the Skopje LC compared with the population figures in 1981 is as in Table 4:

Thus the Macedonians have a considerably higher representation in the LC membership than in the population while the representation of the ethnic minorities, excepting the Serbs, is far below their share in the ethnic composition of the population and this situation is typical of the republic as a whole. The minorities of Macedonia are not keen to join the ruling LC and it appears that the Socialist Republic of Macedonia is a state effectively run by Macedonians — more than their position in the population figures merits.

The fall of Rankovic in 1966 allowed Albanian dissatisfaction in Kosovo to come out into the open and there were large-scale demonstrations in November 1968 calling for Kosovo to be granted republican status, followed by similar demonstrations in Tetovo with the demand for the Albanian areas of Macedonia to join Kosovo in a seventh republic. To grant such a republic is seen, probably correctly, by many Yugoslavs as being merely the first stage in an Albanian plot to eventually separate these areas and to join them with neighbouring Albania. The constitution of 1974, compromised and made Kosovo an Autonomous Province within the Serbian republic with, de facto, many of the powers of a republic within the Yugoslav federation (although recent events, at the time of writing, indicate that this situation has changed with the Serbs reaffirming their control of the security apparatus in Kosovo and even the arrest in March 1989 of the former Kosovo party leader Azem Vllasi, a former protégé of Tito's. Constitutional changes were pushed through in March 1989, limiting Kosovo's autonomy vis-à-vis Serbia proper).

The setting up of an Albanian university in Pristina, the capital of Kosovo, in 1968 and the huge number of Albanian students who enrol there, in part due to the acute

Table 4			
Ethnic group	% of population	% of membership	% of group in LC
Macedonians	67.00	82.95	20.95
Albanians	14.36	5.43	6.39
Serbs	4.88	5.59	19.39
Gypsies	3.59	0.63	2.95
Turks	3.42	1.13	5.57
Muslims (Pomaks)	3.42	0.90	4.44

(Figures from: 'Nationalities in the LCY: Ethnic Composition of the membership of the League of Communists in Major Cities of the Republics and Provinces' by Boris Vuskovic, *Nase Teme*, No.3-4 March-April 1986, Zagreb)

unemployment problem in Kosovo, helped to create a large Albanian intelligentsia with little outlet in terms of job opportunities for them. This dangerous situation helped to fuel nationalist discontent on the part of the Albanians which exploded in 1981 with massive demonstrations, calling again for Kosovo to become a republic, which needed the army to restore order and in which many died — according to official sources nine or 11 people died and several hundred were wounded but unofficial sources estimated far higher casualty figures, and the Central Committee of the League of Communists of Serbia was reportedly told that over 300 people had died in the course of the demonstrations.[54] Since then over 7000 Albanians, mostly young men (students, teachers and even school children), have been arrested and imprisoned in Kosovo for nationalist activity with many receiving prison sentences of six years or more.[55]

There have been similar if smaller scale nationalist manifestations by Albanians in Macedonia and the authorities have become increasingly worried at them and have reacted with, if anything, even greater severity in terms of penal sentencing than in Kosovo. Should such a proposed seventh republic comprising the Albanian dominated areas of Western Macedonia occur, this would severely truncate the 'Macedonian' Republic and almost certainly revive Bulgarian (and even Greek and Serbian) claims to the remaining rump. Thus the growth of Albanian nationalism in Macedonia could prove fatal not only to the territorial integrity of the republic but even to the very existence of the Macedonian nation.

In July 1981 the Macedonian Assembly's Commission for Intra-National Relations backed the demand by the Assembly's Socio-Political Chamber for a revision of syllabuses and textbooks to attempt to stem the rising nationalist tide among Albanians. The Commission called for the number of hours devoted to teaching Macedonian in Albanian language schools to be increased and measures taken to prevent schools from not teaching Macedonian at all. In August 1981 the Macedonian Republican Pedagogical Council in Skopje noted 'weaknesses in the teaching syllabuses, programmes, textbooks and reference works used by the Albanian nationality in Macedonia' and it was stated that 'publishers had been insufficiently vigilant in preventing the penetration of Albanian nationalistic, irredentist and counter-revolutionary tendencies through printed textbooks and other literature' (Tanjug 28 August 1981).

On 7 May 1984 the Macedonian Secretary for Internal Affairs reported that 'activity by the internal enemy from positions of Albanian nationalism and irredentism' had become more pronounced and that 'in 1983 alone, three illegal groups with 11 members, six organizers of leaflet circulation and 15 authors of leaflets with contents from positions of Albanian nationalism and irredentism, were detected in the republic'. A further 'total of 160 persons had been detected making hostile verbal statements'.[56]

On 10 December 1986 *Borba*, the LCY organ published in Belgrade, reported on the increasingly frequent party punishments for 'unvigilant' participations in weddings and other celebrations in the Tetovo area by Albanian officials following a wedding in Strimnica village attended by senior officials at which supposed 'expressions of nationalist euphoria' were present. The same article reported on the findings of Muamer Visko, editor-in-chief of the Albanian-language service broadcast by Radio Skopje. He had apparently listened to the entire record library of Albanian popular tunes and folksongs and from just over 1000 records had found 260 which had 'nationalistic or national-romantic' content — many from the People's Socialist Republic of

Albania and some even recorded by 'Balkanton' in Sofia, Bulgaria. The article went on to point to the dangers of unregistered Albanian artistic societies using unapproved repertoire of nationalist content, especially on local radio stations broadcasting in the Albanian language in Kumanovo, Tetovo, Kicevo, Gostivar, Struga and Resen.

The Macedonian authorities, again with parallels to the Bulgarian authorities' name-changing campaign, also turned their attention to Albanian names. On 17 December 1986 Tanjug reported that a registrar in Tetovo commune was expelled from the LC for registering names 'which stimulated nationalist sentiment and adherence to the People's Socialist Republic of Albania' to newborn Albanian children of 'nationalist inspired parents'. The offending names quoted were Alban, Albana, Shqipe, Fljamur (Albanian flag); Kustrim (call); Ljiriduam (we want freedom); and one meaning 'Red Eagle'. Additionally it was reported that for the names of cities and towns the Macedonian forms, not the Albanian ones, must be used. The banning of Albanian names and Albanian folksongs prompted protests from Albanian writers in Kosovo.

The high birth rate of the Albanian population has also worried the Macedonian authorities and the spectre of expanding 'ethnically pure' Albanian areas akin to the situation developing in Kosovo has apparently promoted them to contemplate punitive administrative measures against those with large families. On 28 January 1988 ATA, the official news agency of the People's Socialist Republic of Albania, using extracts from the Yugoslav newspapers *Rilindja* of Pristina, Kosovo, and *Vecerne Novosti* of Belgrade, accused the Macedonian authorities of 'neo-Malthusian' policies after it was reported that in Tetovo commune a 'package of administrative measures' would be introduced at the beginning of 1988 to restrain births. Among the measures are that families should pay for medical services of any children more than the ideal two in number and that there would be no child allowance for such extra children, and even a possible financial penalty. ATA reported that these measures are also to be introduced in the communes of Gostivar, Debar, Kicevo and Struga.

The campaign against Albanian nationalism, called 'differentiation', has escalated. On 25 October 1987 *Flaka e Vellazerimit*, published in Albanian in Skopje, reported the decision by the President of the Tetovo LC Municipal Committee to apparently dismiss a further 100 Albanian officials from the state administration and subject them to 'ideological differentiation' and the same paper reported on 30 October of measures taken by the Republican Secretariat for People's Defence against 34 Albanian officers in Tetovo commune, most of whom apparently were discharged for attending Albanian weddings at which 'nationalist' songs were sung. Many cultural clubs have also been disbanded.

These and other measures, which go even further than the anti-Albanian nationalism policies of 'differentiation' in Kosovo, have provoked opposition from within the League of Communists, especially from the Albanian members in Kosovo which have in turn angered the Macedonian members. The delegates at the Macedonian Assembly session in February 1988 reacted sharply to criticism of Macedonian policies by Azem Vllasi, then President of the Kosovo LC Provincial Committee but at the time of writing arrested on charges of anti-state activity due to the current Serbian backlash against Albanian nationalism. The Assembly agreed that the legal measures — 'above all, the provisions concerning personal names, the ban on the sale of property in the western part of the republic [to prevent Albanians buying out Macedonians and creating "ethnically pure territories"], the amendment to the law on religious teaching [to prohibit the attendance of organized religious instruction by young people up to the age of 15], and the resolution on population policy, whose purpose is to stop aggressive demographic expansion' — was 'to prevent the activities of Albanian nationalists and separatists'.[57]

For the Albanian population in Macedonia it is perhaps events in the field of education and language rights which have provoked the most opposition. In 1983 teachers in Tetovo were disciplined and some dismissed from the LC for not observing regulations regarding the use of Macedonian in official matters and Tanjug on 5 October 1983 reported that 'a large number of pupils of Albanian nationality also followed their teacher's example by boycotting and belittling the Macedonian language'. A law on secondary school education of 1985 in Macedonia stipulated that classes with Albanian as the language of instruction can only be created if over 30 Albanian pupils enrol for the class and there are enough qualified teachers. This law has become progressively more strictly enforced, resulting in the closure of classes with an insufficient intake of Albanian pupils and compelling Albanians to attend mixed classes with the instruction in Macedonian. The impact of the enforcement of this law is that while in 1981 there were 8200 pupils attending classes in secondary schools in Albanian, by the end of 1988 the newspaper *Oslobodjenje* published in Sarajevo reported on 6 January 1989 that the figure was down to 4221.

Although some of the 'missing' pupils can be explained by the impact on secondary schools of the growing numbers of Albanian children who are failing to attend primary school — on 8 October 1987 Tanjug reported that in 1986 criminal proceedings were initiated in 3802 cases in the municipalities of Gostivar, Tetovo, Skopje, Struga, Kichevo, Titov Veles and Kumanovo almost always against Albanians — the compulsory schooling in Macedonian for some Albanian pupils has caused great resentment and boycotts, such as the boycott by 60 Albanian pupils in September 1987 at the Nace Budjoni centre for vocational training in Kumanovo. Albanians have also claimed that the apparent lack of qualified Albanian teachers leading to the closure of classes is due to the dismissal of many teachers for allegedly indoctrinating their pupils with Albanian nationalism — according to official sources at least 150 teachers were dismissed in 1988. The problems involved were highlighted by the fact that, according to a Tanjug report of 10 September 1987, some of the pupils did not know Macedonian and therefore were unable to follow mixed classes in it. Albanian teachers also protested at the measures and at the Nace Bugjoni and Pero Nakov centres in Kumanovo nine teachers and 26 pupils were expelled. Similar events took place in Gostivar.

The situation boiled over in 1988 with demonstrations by young Albanians in Kumanovo in August, and Gostivar in October, holding banners and shouting slogans against the measures and claiming their rights as guaranteed in the 1974 Constitution. In Kumanovo at least 128 Albanians were detained for up to 60 days and the authorities responded by arresting in both instances the organizers, 20 of whom were subsequently imprisoned. For example in January in the district court of Skopje, three men aged 32, 29 and 19 were sentenced to between six and 11 years' imprisonment and four minors aged 16 or 17, two of whom were girls and all of whom were pupils at the Pance Popovski school in Gostivar, received sentences of between four and six years' imprisonment for their part in the Gostivar demonstration.

Apart from the dissatisfaction relating to education, there were also protests in 1988 by Albanians in Kumanovo and elsewhere in Macedonia at the official demolition of the traditional high walls around ethnic Albanian houses.

Macedonian officials have stated that such demolitions were required by urban planning. However Albanians claim that the real reason is an attack on traditional Albanian culture and has also caused economic hardship as the walls are used for drying tobacco, the main, and sometimes the only, source of income for families.

The situation in Kosovo, always closely watched by all Albanians in Macedonia and often an important pointer to future action in Macedonia, has deteriorated. There were demonstrations in November 1988 at the resignation under Serbian pressure of Azem Vllasi, the then Kosovo leader, and his removal from the Central Committee of the League of Communists of Yugoslavia for ostensibly encouraging Albanian nationalism. He was subsequently arrested allegedly for anti-state activity. Matters took a decided turn for the worse in February 1989 when troops were sent into the province after a general strike by Albanians in protest at proposed constitutional changes limiting the province's autonomy within the republic of Serbia. In March the changes were passed leading to clashes between demonstrators and troops in which at least 24 people — unofficial sources cite over 100 — died. Amnesty International reported that more than 800 demonstrators including school pupils were summarily imprisoned for up to 60 days and many others held pending more serious charges. Up to 2000 miners and other workers have been jailed for up to 60 days or fined, sacked or disciplined for taking industrial action and some 200 others have had their passports withdrawn. Journalists, teachers and party members have been purged and an unknown number of school pupils who took part in the demonstrations have been expelled from school.[58]

Religion

The Albanians of Macedonia are overwhelmingly Muslims with a few Orthodox villages around Lake Ohrid and a small number of Roman Catholics in Skopje most of whom have moved from the Prizren area in the neighbouring province of Kosovo. Some observers have held that Islam is not held in high esteem among the Albanians of Yugoslavia and that most *hodzhas* oppose the growth of Albanian nationalism. However in Macedonia the authorities see Islam as a tool of Albanian nationalism and as a way for the Albanians to assimilate other smaller Islamic minority groups, like the Turks and Pomaks and Muslim Gypsies. This was detailed in a 23 page instalment published by the Skopje daily *Vecer* between 25 September and 21 October 1980 entitled 'Islamism in Macedonia'. An article in *Nova Makedonija*, published in Skopje on 19 June 1981, whilst reporting on the rejection by the Macedonian Islamic community of Albanian nationalism noted that in some villages where Muslim Macedonians live *hodzhas* who preach in Albanian had been appointed. On 21 December 1986, *NIN*, a magazine published in Belgrade, commented on the large number of Albanians from Macedonia undergoing religious instruction in Arab countries and the same article stated that in the preceding 10 years there had been 210 mosques renovated or built in Western Macedonia.

There have been a number of subsequent articles and reports about 'too extensive' Islamic religious instruction in Macedonia and how the Islamic community in Macedonia is overstepping the legal regulations, especially regarding instruction to under-age girls. This last point is highlighted by the problem of the Teteks clothing factory in Pirok, just outside Tetovo, in recruiting women employees despite some 20,000 unemployed Albanian women in and around Tetovo, thereby necessitating the commuting of over 200 workers daily from Skopje.[59] Local Albanians however see such 'busing-in' of non-Albanian labour as another example of the authorities anti-Albanian policies. The authorities blame Islamic doctrination of women and traditional Albanian attitudes to women and have been loathe to cooperate in allowing new mosques to be opened. For example in 1983 authorization was sought for the erection of a minaret, financed privately by the Albanian inhabitants, in the village of Donja Arnakija, but was refused. The villagers went ahead with the construction but in December 1986 the minaret was dynamited by the authorities.[60] As noted above, the authorities have also amended the law on religious teaching to prohibit the attendance of organized religious instruction by young people up to the age of 15 specifically to counter the growing influence of Islam. Conversely the authorities have good relations with the Macedonian Orthodox Church which is seen as a standard bearer of the Macedonian nation in the ethnically mixed areas of Western Macedonia.

Communities apart

The reality of the situation in Macedonia is that there is very little mixing between ethnic groups. A study published in 1974 by the sociologist Dr. Ilija Josifovski[61] on the Macedonian, Albanian and Turkish populations in the villages of Polog which includes the areas around Tetovo and Gostivar showed that 95% of the Albanian and Macedonian and 84% of the Turkish heads of individual households would not let their sons marry a girl of different nationality while for daughters the figures were even higher. For Albanians this is shown by the numbers of Albanian students at Skopje University whose sisters attend Pristina University in Kosovo which is almost entirely Albanian in intake and where they will meet only Albanian men. Mixed marriages between Macedonians on one hand and Albanians and Turks on the other were found not to exist in the study. Religion was again seen as being of paramount importance and that 'a religious isolation stands behind the deceptive impression of national, ethnic cleavages'.

The drift from village to town among the Macedonian population is shown by a 42% decline in agricultural population over the period 1963 to 1971 while for the same period the Albanian agricultural population declined by only 11%, again similar to the differences between Slavs and ethnic Turks in Bulgaria, so that many Macedonian villages are now populated almost entirely by the old despite the authorities offering financial inducements for young Macedonians either to stay in the villages or return to them. These declining communities and the new villages of 'Weekendicas' — holiday homes for the Macedonian well-to-do which are empty during the week — contrasts greatly with the Albanian and Gypsy (and Muslim Macedonian) villages with their numbers of youths and children readily visible on the streets.

Thus despite the aim of 'Brotherhood and Unity' the picture is one of mistrust and increasing alienation between the Macedonians and the rapidly expanding Albanian population of Macedonia mirrored in everyday relations by chauvinist attitudes from both sides.

The Turks

Assessing the number of minorities like the Turks and others (see below) in Macedonia is somewhat problematic. The census of 1948 gave 95,940 Turks while that of 1953 recorded 203,938 and yet by the next census seven years later the number was only 131,481. Immediately after World War II the Turks had been seen as suspect due to friendship between Turkey and the West and, in Janury 1948, 17 Macedonian Turks were tried as members of *Judzel* — ostensibly a terrorist/espionage organization. The trial was given great publicity within Macedonia so as to intimidate the Turkish minority, and as a result many Turks declared themselves to be Albanians in the 1948 census. However by 1953, following the break by Yugoslavia with the Cominform, the Albanians were now seen as being suspect and therefore many Albanians declared themselves to be Turks — of the 203,938 in the 1953 census, 32,392 gave Macedonian as their native tongue and 27,086 gave Albanian, and the number of declared Albanians fell from 179,389 in 1948 to 165,524 in 1963. The period following 1953 saw extensive emigration to Turkey of large numbers of Yugoslavia's Turkish minority — some 80,000 according to figures from Yugoslavia's statistical yearbooks, or over 150,000 according to some Turkish sources. However some of these emigrants were unable to speak any Turkish and were in fact Muslim Albanians who, fearing for their position in post-war communist Yugoslavia, claimed to be Turks so as to take advantage of the permitted emigration.[62]

In the 1971 census there were 108,552 Turks and by the census of 1981 their numbers had apparently dropped to 86,690. Such a decline is more surprising given the high birth rate of the Turks in Yugoslavia which would have been expected to result in an increase of some 20,000 in the period 1971/81 instead of a decrease of over 20,000. It appears that many who previously declared themselves to be Turks now call themselves Moslems while others now declare themselves to be Albanians or Gypsies. A further complicating factor in assessing numbers of the smaller minority groups in Macedonia is the rise from 3,652 to 14,240 between 1971 and 1981 of those declaring themselves to be Yugoslavs rather than as belonging to a particular ethnic group, although the percentage of those declaring themselves as such is still low in comparison to other republics in Yugoslavia.

The Macedonian authorities, worried at the rise of Albanian nationalism, assert that many Turks have been Albanianized under pressure. According to the director of the Macedonian Republic Bureau of Statistics in Skopje[63] this was especially pronounced in the Tetovo, Gostivar, Struga and Kicevo regions and the Macedonian LC Central Committee Presidium in September 1987 gave the expansion of Albanian nationalism as one of the main reasons for the emigration of Turkish families from Gostivar municipality.[64] The Albanians apparently claim, in a manner strikingly similar to the Bulgarian government vis-à-vis ethnic Turks in Bulgaria, that 'these are not Turks' but actually 'Illyrians [believed to be the forerunners of the Albanians] turned into Turks' who are now 'returning to their flock'.[65]

Similarly to the Albanians, the Turks, a recognized nationality of Yugoslavia, have been allowed educational and cultural rights from the outset — in the first academic year of the new republic, 1944/5, there were 60 primary schools with 3,334 pupils using Turkish as the language of instruction. In 1950/51 there were over 100 schools with over 12,000 pupils and 267 teachers. By 1958/9, due to the emigration to Turkey, the numbers had dropped to 27 schools (26 primary and one secondary) with just over 6000 pupils and 219 teachers[66] and while the number of primary schools had increased to 53 by the end of 1988 the number of pupils has remained more or less the same.[67] Again, like the Albanians, there are television and radio programmes and a newspaper, *Birlik*, as well as various cultural organizations and the like.

The Muslim Macedonians

This apparent confusion over identity of the different Muslim groups shows again that in the Balkans religion has often been of paramount importance in ethnic differentiation. This is illustrated by the Muslim

Macedonians, known as **Torbeshes**, **Pomaks**, or **Poturs**. Similarly to the Pomaks in Bulgaria these Muslims often in the past showed greater identification with fellow Muslims, especially Turks, although as noted above the authorities have been worried at the penetration of Albanian nationalism into this community by way of, among other things, Albanian-speaking hodzhas. The numbers of these Slav Muslims has fluctuated greatly in past censuses — 1591 in 1953; 3002 in 1961; 1248 in 1971; and a dramatic rise to 39,555 in 1981. This last figure presumably includes many who previously declared themselves as Turks.

These Slav Muslims formed themselves into an association and held their first historical, cultural meeting in 1970 at the monastery of Saint Jovan Bigorski in Western Macedonia. This association claims that over 70,000 of their number have been assimilated by other Muslim groups since the war, especially the Albanians.[68] If this has been the case, then the rise in their number as reflected in the 1981 census shows that the founding of the association has been very successful.

The Gypsies

Since 1981 the Gypsies in Yugoslavia — some 850,000 in total — have been granted the status of a nationality of Yugoslavia although Macedonia had in the 1981 census apparently still designated them as an ethnic group (a lower status in Yugoslavia's three-tier ethnic ranking of nation, nationality of Yugoslavia, and other nationalities or ethnic group). Their numbers in the censuses remained more or less static until the last census of 1981 when they rose dramatically from 24,505 to 43,223 reflecting their greater official status and a decline in stigma attached to being a Gypsy in Yugoslavia. The Gypsies still however suffer from severe discrimination and come behind Albanians and Turks in the queue for jobs — often Gypsy women are employed as domestic helps for low wages with no health benefits despite labour laws which outlaw such employment. Despite increased representation in local municipal councils and in the Macedonian Assembly, society at large has a noticeably racist attitude to the Gypsy population.

However progress has been made. In Skopje the cultural associaton *Phralipe* (Brotherhood) was founded in 1948 and the realization of their rights as a nationality of Yugoslavia has meant regular broadcasts in Romanes from Tetovo and in the neighbouring province of Kosovo, where the breakthrough in the introduction of Romanes into the education system occurred, there is a weekly television programme in Romanes which many of the population can tune into. The most significant feature, however, is the Gypsy town of Suto Orizari, comprising some 35,000 inhabitants, with its own elected council and delegate to the Assembly, outside Skopje. This town enjoys a higher standard of living than many Macedonian villages. Overall the position of the Gypsy population in Macedonia, as in Yugoslavia generally, is rising albeit from a very low starting level.[69]

The Vlachs

There is very little information on the situation regarding this ethnic group which speaks a form of Romanian and traditionally comprised of pastoral people in Western Macedonia. They live primarily in Greece and in Yugoslavia. Assessing their numbers is difficult and compounded by a lack of a separatist current among Vlachs, also known as **Koutsovlachs**, **Aromani** and **Cincari** in Yugoslavia, which has resulted in their apparent peaceful assimilation into majority ethnic groups. In this shared religious faith, Orthodoxy, has been an important factor. The Vlachs in Macedonia live especially in and around Bitola, Resen and Krusevo. There are Vlach societies in Bitola and Skopje and these societies have pointed to the lack of language rights for Vlachs in schools and in religious matters — e.g. the appeal in February 1988 by the Pitu Guli Cultural Association in Skopje to the Foreign Ministers of Yugoslavia, Albania, Bulgaria, Greece, Romania and Turkey who were meeting in Belgrade — but with little apparent effect. Successive censuses have shown a gradual decline in their numbers in Macedonia from 8669 in 1953 to 6392 in 1981, and it appears that they are becoming assimilated by the majority Macedonian population.

Studies in the 1930s recorded 3-4000 Vlachs in Bitola, 2-3000 in Skopje and 1500 in Krusevo which was predominately Vlach at the time; however recent studies, especially those by Jovan Trifonoski, show a pattern of gradual assimilation. Using the Ovce Polje area in the east of the republic as a case study[70] he showed how the Vlachs in this area originated from Gramos in southern Albania but emigrated to Macedonia at the end of the 18th century to escape the tyranny of Ali Pasha of Janjina. They were nomadic cattle breeders and maintained an extended family under a dominant headman, summering in the mountains of Osgovo, Pljackovica and Ograzden, and wintering in the plains of Strumica, Kocan, Ovce Polje and as far as Thessaloniki. After the First World War new boundaries and new economics induced a shift from nomadic flocks to farming due to the disintegration of the old Turkish estates and the narrowing down of pastures. This trend was amplified after World War II as after 1948 under the new economic system big flocks of sheep or horses could not be owned. Most Vlachs abandoned their nomadic life and settled in existing villages; they already were well acquainted with the areas from winter dwellings previously. Others from Ovce Polje settled in surrounding areas: Stip, Kocani, Titov Veles but often moved back to the Ovce Polje area after 1948 when land became available due to the complete emigration of Turks in the area. A result of this was contact between the Vlach cultures on one hand and the indigenous Macedonian/Slavic culture on the other. Even in 1938 it was noted that nomadic Vlachs living in the Ograzden mountains could speak Slav well, including the women, and some children were attending schools. In 1971 Trifunoski noted that the Vlachs of Eastern Macedonia living in the mass of the Slavic population were fading away as a separate group and the growth of industry in Titov Veles, Stip and Skopje with the attendant mass emigration of the young from the villages has further escalated this process.

Aegean Macedonia and Thrace (Greece)

The Macedonians

As noted above the Greek authorities have from the outset of the modern Greek state consistently denied the existence of the Slav Macedonians as a separate people from the Greeks and instead officially referred to them as Slavophone Greeks while the Bulgarians claimed them to be Bulgarians — in common speech the Greek population referred to them as Bulgarians and the notion of them as a separate people, the Macedonians, only really came later. Assessing population figures is problematic due to the tendency to exaggerate the number of the Greek or Slav populations depending on which side is making the assessment — the Greeks, the Bulgarians or the Yugoslavs. One of the most detailed assessments is a Yugoslav one,[71] using Bulgarian and Greek sources, just before the Balkan Wars of 1912, which saw the liberation of the areas from Ottoman rule, that there were in Aegean Macedonia: 326,426 Macedonians; 40,921 Muslim Macedonians (Pomaks); 289,973 Turks; 4240 Christian Turks; 2112 Cherkez (Mongols); 240,019 Greeks; 13,753 Muslim Greeks; 5584 Muslim Albanians; 3291 Christian Albanians; 45,457 Vlachs; 3500 Muslim Vlachs; 59,560 Jews; 29,803 Gypsies; and 8100 others making a total of 1,073,549 inhabitants.

However from 1913 to 1926 there were large-scale changes in the population structure due to ethnic migrations. During and immediately after the Balkan Wars about 15,000 Slavs left the new Greek territories for Bulgaria while many Greeks from Thrace, Pirin and Vardar Macedonia moved to be under Greek rule. More significant was the Greek-Bulgarian convention of 27 November 1919 which allowed voluntary population exchange in which some 25,000 Greeks left Bulgaria for Greece and between 52,000 and 72,000 (depending on which estimate is used[72]). Slavs left Greece for Bulgaria, mostly from Eastern Aegean Macedonia which from then onwards remained virtually free of Slavs. Most Slavs living west of the Vardar river, especially bordering on Yugoslavia, chose to remain. Greece was obliged to protect its Slav minorities and these obligations were further stipulated in the Treaty of Sèvres in 1920 with educational rights and guarantees for the use of their mother tongue for official purposes. In September 1924 Greece and Bulgaria signed a protocol known as the Kalfov-Politis Agreement which placed the 'Bulgarian' minority in Greece under the protection of the League of Nations which prompted the Yugoslavs to renounce the Greek-Serbian treaty of 1913 in protest. On 15 January 1925 Greece announced that they would not follow the protocol and henceforth treated the Slavs as Greeks. In 1926 the Greek government ordered in Decree No.332 of November 1926 that all Slavonic names of towns, villages, rivers and mountains should be replaced by Greek ones.[73]

Up until the Balkan Wars there were in Aegean Macedonia under the control of the Exarchate Church 19 primary schools in towns and 186 in villages with 320 teachers catering for 12,895 pupils in Bulgarian. In addition there were four Serbian schools and some 200 or so other Slav primary schools supported by village communities. All these Slavonic schools were closed and the inventories destroyed while in the Slavonic churches the icons were repainted with Greek names.[74]

Larger population exchanges took place between Greece and Turkey following the Greco-Turkish War of 1920-22. The peace treaty of July 1924 stipulated that the Greek and Turkish populations of Turkey and Greece respectively were to be exchanged, except for the Greeks of Istanbul and the Turks of Western Thrace. Again, as so often in the Balkans, religion was the criteria used to define 'Greek' or 'Turk'

which resulted in many non-Turkish Muslims (Slavs and Greeks) emigrating to Turkey and conversely Turkish-speaking Christians to Greece. In this exchange some 390,000 Muslims (mostly Turks) emigrated to Turkey and over 1,200,000 Greeks left Turkey of whom some 540,000 settled in Aegean Macedonia along with about 100,000 more Greek refugees who had come before 1920. Thus there was an influx of over 600,000 Greek refugees into Aegean Macedonia while the Turkish and Pomak population outside of Western Thrace mostly emigrated. The official Greek census of 1928 recorded 1,237,000 Greeks; 82,000 Slavophones; and 93,000 others, although this census almost certainly exaggerated the number of Greeks.

The position of the Macedonian minority worsened in the period 1936-41 under the Metaxas regime which viewed the minority as a danger to Greece's security. Yugoslav sources allege that over 5000 Macedonians were interned from the border regions with Yugoslavia, and night schools were opened to teach adult Macedonians the Greek language.[75] The repression was further stepped up after the beginning of the Greco-Italian War in October 1940, despite the numbers of Macedonians fighting loyally in Greece's armies, with, according to Yugoslav sources, some 1600 Macedonians interned on the islands of Thasos and Kefallinia (Cephalonia).[76]

After the defeat of Greece by the Axis powers in 1941, Bulgaria occupied the eastern portion of Greek Aegean Macedonia, excepting Salonika which was occupied by the Germans, and a small part of the western portion. The remainder was under the Italians. In the portions under Bulgarian rule the Bulgarians imported settlers from Bulgaria and acted such that even a German report of the time described the Bulgarian occupation as 'a regime of terror which can only be described as "Balkan" '. In Kavalla alone over 700 shops and enterprises were expropriated and large numbers of Greeks expelled or deprived of their right to work by a licence system that banned the practice of a trade or profession without permission from the occupying authorities.[77] The Bulgarians acted with such ruthlessness that the Greek population, many of whom were previously emigres from Turkey and who were understandably hostile to being once more ruled by a foreign power, became bitterly anti-Bulgarian. Thus Bulgaria, in the brief period when she finally controlled some of the areas in Aegean Macedonia she always claimed, succeeded in alienating the populations under its control in while losing influence to the Yugoslavs in Western Aegean Macedonia.

Another product of the brutal Bulgarian rule was that the Greek population became more violently opposed than ever to the idea of a 'United Macedonia' which, up until the change of line of the Comintern in the mid-1930s to that of the Popular Fronts following Hitler's rise to power, had been the Greek Communist Party's (KKE) line. This line, which was always unpopular with rank and file Greeks, was resumed by the Communist-controlled resistance movement The National Liberation Front, EAM, and its military wing, ELAS, and in 1943 EAM- ELAS tried to organize resistance in Aegean Macedonia. Tito's aide Vukmanovic-Tempo, who was very successful in Yugoslav Vardar Macedonia, set up SNOF, the Slav National Liberation Front, which comprised of Macedonian Slav Partisan units allied to ELAS but this provoked prolonged resistance from non-Communist Greeks, especially from a movement called 'the Protectors of Northern Greece' (YVE), and relations between ELAS and SNOF were strained.

The Greek civil war which began in earnest in late 1946, after a brief 'First Round' in the winter of 1943/4, and 'Second Round' in December 1944, between the Communist-controlled ELAS and non-Communists supported by Britain and later the USA, saw the exodus of many Slavs and Greek Communist Party members fleeing to Yugoslavia. The last round of the civil war which lasted until 1949 saw SNOF reformed as NOF (National Liberation Front) and up to 40% of the Communist forces comprising of Macedonians. However the struggle at the top of the KKE between Nikos Zachariades and Markos Vafiadis, who had close links with Tito which even survived the initial Stalin-Tito break of 1948, and which ended in Markos's retirement due to 'ill-health' on 31 January 1949, was followed by an attempt by the KKE to set up an anti-Tito NOF but by now the war was virtually lost for the Communists and only gestures remained. On 1 March 1949 'Free Greece', the communist radio station, broadcasted a declaration of an Independent United Macedonia which was not recognized by the Soviet Union or its allies and only caused alarm in the rank and file of the KKE. In July 1949 Tito closed the Yugoslav-Greek frontier.

During World War II and the ensuing civil war the Slavs of Aegean Macedonia enjoyed language rights such as education in Slavonic which had been denied them before except for the brief appearance of a Slavonic primer, *Abecedar*, in September 1925.[78]

In the period after the civil war the Macedonians were, unsurprisingly, seen as potentially disloyal to the Greek state and steps were taken to try and remove such 'undesirable aliens' from the sensitive border regions with Yugoslavia. In 1953 Decree No.2536 was enacted to colonize the northern territories 'with new colonists with healthy national consciousness'[79] — the anti-Macedonian element in this law was evident by the exclusion of the Turks in Western Thrace from such measures.[80] In this period it was forbidden for Macedonians to use the Slavonic forms for their names and henceforth only Greek forms could be used for official purposes — a measure with obvious parallels to recent Bulgarian measures against its minorities. In the beginning of 1954 the Papagos government resolved to remove all Macedonians from official posts in Aegean Macedonia. In the border regions with Yugoslavia peasants were not allowed to move from their villages and in 1959 in the villages around Lerin, Kostur and Kajlari the inhabitants were asked to confirm publicly in front of officials that they did not speak Macedonian. Such measures led to many emigrating to Australia or Canada.[81]

Since the civil war, the official denial of a Macedonian minority in Greece has remained constant regardless of the government in power and the military dictatorship of 1967-74 saw a worsening of the minority situation with many Macedonians interned or imprisoned. The return to democracy in Greece saw an improvement with the abandonment of official terror. However the education system and the lack of job opportunities for those who declared themselves to be Macedonian in any branch of the state bureaucracy have greatly aided assimilation into the Greek majority and the Greek authorities have apparently been successful in going a long way towards achieving this aim. It is noticeable that Macedonian nationalism appears much stronger in emigres from Aegean Macedonia, not merely in Yugoslavia but also Australia or Canada, than in the area itself. The massive dilution of the Macedonian population by emigration on the one hand and influx of Greeks on the other combined with the experience of the civil war has made the aim some kind of Macedonian state incorporating Aegean Macedonia merely a dream shared by a few.

Refugees and relations between Greece, Yugoslavia and Bulgaria

A continuing legacy of the civil war has been the numbers of people who fled from Greece including some 25,000-30,000, according to the Association of Refugee Children from Aegean Macedonia and Red Cross estimates, of children aged between two and 14 — the Greek government alleged that many of these children were virtually kidnapped by Communists but the number of parents requesting Red Cross help for their return was relatively small.[82] Many of these refugees were Macedonians who went to Yugoslavia or other East European Communist countries. From 1955 onwards Yugoslavia made efforts to attract the refugees from other countries to Yugoslav Macedonia. *Borba*, published in Belgrade on 6 June 1988, stated that there were 150,000 such people who were full citizens of Yugoslavia, however other Yugoslav sources put the numbers of Macedonians who emigrated in the period 1945-9 from Aegean Macedonia as only some 40-50,000 out of a total of 60-70,000. Again there appears to be confusion about actual numbers as there is about the numbers of Macedonians in Aegean Macedonia at present: some Yugoslav sources allege a figure of 350,000 but more reliable estimates are about 200,000.

The property of these refugees was confiscated by the Greek government by Decree 2536/53 which also deprived them of their Greek citizenship.[83] The Greek government later enacted a law so that the property would be returned to refugees who are 'Greek by birth' — i.e. to those who renounce their Macedonian identity and adopt Greek names.[84] Greece also has consistently denied entry visas to these refugees except in a few cases to attend funerals etc. but even then with difficulty. In July 1988, following a reunion in Skopje, over 100 of these former refugees attempted to visit Northern Greece but were turned back at the border after Greek officials refused entry to some of them, and one participant at the reunion, Lefter Lajovski, who was by then a Canadian citizen, claimed that the authorities had asked him to change his name to a Greek one if he wanted to enter Greece, even though no visa is required for Canadian citizens.[85]

Such actions by the Greek government against Macedonians and the Yugoslav Socialist Republic of Macedonia escalated after Andreas Papandreou and his Greek Socialist Party (PASOK) came to power in Greece. Skopje's *Kiril i Metodija* university was taken off the list of foreign academic institutions whose degrees are recognized by Greece as the instruction at the university was in a language, Macedonian, not 'internationally recognized'.[86] Greece repeatedly refused Yugoslavia's initiatives to bilaterally abolish visas and while Serbs, Croats or other Yugoslav nationals have few problems, Tanjug on 12 July 1984 reported that the Greek Consulate in Skopje was asking for special proof from Macedonian entry visa applicants that they were not born in Aegean Macedonia. Papandreou himself has explicitly denied the existence of a Macedonian minority in Greece and has stated that he would not accept any dialogue on this matter.[87] An example of the lengths to which this is drawn is the last minute cancellation in September 1987, when the players were already on court and 5000 spectators present, of a friendly basketball match between Aris of Thessalonika and Metalno Zavod Tito of Skopje due, according to the Skopje paper *Vecer* of 1 October 1987, to the letter 'M' in the name of the Skopje team being seen by the Minister for Northern Greece as standing for Macedonia.

The main Greek conservative party, *Nea Demokratia*, has also continued its hostility to Macedonia and set up in early 1986 a monitoring centre in Florina to monitor broadcasts from Skopje for anti-Yugoslav commentaries. Papandreou himself was attacked by some Greek newspapers for travelling to Yugoslavia in January 1986 'at a time of an allegedly stepped up Yugoslav propaganda drive concerning the so-called Macedonian question' and the Greek newspaper *Stohos* (an extremist small circulation newspaper) which is very nationalistic on minority matters and has alleged that Greek students in Skopje have been pressured to declare themselves as Macedonians, urged Greeks to fight with all available means against those who speak Slavo-Macedonian.[88]

Relations between the Papandreou government and Bulgaria, on the other hand, were very good. It appears that the Bulgarians have acquiesced to the loss of Aegean Macedonia to Greece and united with Greece in denying the existence of a Macedonian nation as espoused by the Yugoslavs — the Bulgarians even going as far as to exclude from Bulgarian television the Yugoslav entry, a Macedonian song, to the 1988 Eurovision song contest along with the Turkish and Israeli entries.[89] The shared problem of enmity to Turkey and Turkish minorities is another factor in the present Greek-Bulgarian friendship well illustrated by the visit by the Greek foreign minister to Sofia and subsequent public thanks to Bulgaria, a Warsaw Pact member, for its support in 1988 during a confrontation with Turkey, ostensibly Greece's NATO ally over territorial problems in the Aegean. The Greeks apparently do not react with the same outrage as the Yugoslavs to the perennial Bulgarian statements about the 'unjust' annullment of the 'Greater Bulgaria' of the San Stefano treaty of 1878 which included present-day Greek as well as Yugoslav Macedonia, and the Greeks do not claim historical events like the Ilinden rising of 1903 as both the Bulgarians and Macedonians do. Neither do Bulgarians antagonize the Greeks by making films like 'The Rescue' which won the highest Bulgarian honour, the Dimitrov prize, in 1986 and which claimed that the population of Ohrid in 1944 was Bulgarian.

The Turks and Pomaks

Assessing the number of **Turks**, and other minorities, in Greece is problematic. The census of 1928 recorded 191,254 Turks while the 1951 census recorded 179,895 Turks of whom virtually all were either Muslim by religion, 92,219, or Orthodox, 86,838. While some live on the Greek islands neighbouring Turkey, most live in Western Thrace. The **Pomaks**, Muslim Slavs or a small number of Muslim Greeks, tend to live also in Western Thrace in villages in the southern Rhodope and due to the official reticence to give figures for ethnic minorities, only for religious ones, it is hard to separate them from the Turks; however the villages near the Bulgarian border in all three provinces of Western Thrace are predominately Pomak with the exception of some, like Mikron Dereion, which have a mixed population of ethnic Turks, Pomaks and Greek Orthodox, or others which have a sedentary Muslim Gypsy population. Many Pomaks also live in Komotini and Xanthi and some also live in Dhidimotikhon. Official Greek sources tend to claim that the Turks are Pomaks or Muslim Greeks while conversely the Turks claim the Pomaks as Turks.

Estimates from the Information Office at the Greek embassy in London based on the 1981 census figures give a total of 110,000 people belonging to religious minorities of whom some 60,000 are Turkish-speaking Muslims; 30,000 Pomaks; and 20,000 Athingani (descendants of Christian heretics expelled from Asia Minor during Byzantine rule) or Gypsies. However Turkish Muslim sources from Western Thrace claim a total of 100,000-120,000 Turkish-speaking Muslims in Western Thrace and most observers estimate between 100,000 and 120,000 Muslims out of a total of some 360,000 in Western Thrace recorded in the census of 1971. Of the other minorities there are small populations of Gagauz, Christian Turkish-speaking people, for example around the city of Alexandroupolis, and Sarakatsani, Greek-speaking transhumants, especially in the village of Palladion. Fieldwork by F. De Jong in 1979[90] to whom much of the above is indebted, notes that there are no longer any Circassians in Western Thrace.

Turkey is Greece's traditional enemy, despite being a NATO pact partner, and similarly to Bulgaria, Greece fears Turkish expansion, especially after the example of Cyprus and huge posters, featuring a bleeding partitioned Cyprus with appropriate captions, were openly displayed in Thrace in 1987. Much of Western Thrace is a restricted area due to reasons of national security. These areas are the border regions with Bulgaria where many Turks and Pomaks live and in these militarized areas large portions of land have been expropriated from Pomaks and Turks and the inhabitants are severely restricted in their freedom of movement to 30 kms. radius of their residence. Decree 1366/1938 which forbids foreign nationals to buy land near border areas is still operational and it is claimed that this decree is used against ethnic Turks and Pomaks even though they are Greek citizens.

In the exchange of population following the Greco-Turkish War of 1920-22 some 60,000 Greek refugees from Asia Minor were allowed, in contravention to the Treaty of Lausanne, to settle in Western Thrace and under steady administrative and economic pressure from the Greek authorities a gradual migration of Muslims to Turkey ensued; this is particularly noticeable in the previously Muslim province of Ebros where the population now is Greek Orthodox. World War II and the civil war saw a rise in the number of such emigres and some 20,000 left for Turkey in the period 1939-51 with emigration continuing to the present day.

The deterioration of relations with Turkey over the developing situation in Cyprus saw a corresponding deterioration of the situation of the Turkish minority in Western Thrace with increased pressure to induce emigration. At the same time the Turkish government began to raise the issue of the minority as a counterpoise to Greek claims for uniting Cyprus with Greece (successive Greek governments have tended to see any complaints from Turks in Western Thrace as being orchestrated by Turkey and have also pointed to the unhappy situation of the 100,000 or so Greeks allowed under the Treaty of Lausanne to remain in Istanbul who have suffered severe harassment and whose numbers have declined drastically as a result to under 10,000 by 1974 and whose position seems serious in the extreme.[91]) Under the military dictatorship of 1967-74 the situation worsened. Members of the Turkish minority community boards, elected under provision of Decree 2345/1920, were dismissed and replaced by non-elected people, appointed by government agencies, prepared to act contrary to the interests of the Muslim community. Examples are the appointment, without any qualifications, of a Gypsy Muslim, Ahmet Damatoglu, previously an imam, as Mufti of Dhidhimotikon (Dimotoka) in 1973, and a non-Muslim as chairman of the council for the administration of religious organizations in Xanthi in 1967. In this period Greeks, including many Sarakatsani — a Greek-speaking transhumant people akin to the Vlachs — were given financial inducement to move into Western Thrace to dilute the Muslim Turkish-speaking population. Despite the return to democracy in 1974 the trend continued aided by Greek reaction to the Turkish invasion of Cyprus. There has been no return to the former democratic practices as stipulated in Decree 2345/1920 and when the Mufti of Komotini died on 2 July 1985 he was replaced by a government appointee. When the new Mufti resigned almost immediately due to community protests he was replaced six months later by another appointee without consultation. Since 1977 all the place names in Komotini were changed from Turkish forms to Greek forms and henceforth it was forbidden to use the old names for official purposes, apparently on pain of fines or even imprisonment. Mention of the Turkish name in parenthesis after the Greek names is also forbidden.[92]

Over a long period there have been growing complaints by Muslims, Turks and Pomaks, that they, unlike Greek Orthodox Christians, cannot buy real estate, except for a few select people who cooperate with the authorities, neither can they negotiate loans or credits; that building construction for Turkish houses has been withheld for many years resulting in the Turks being forced to live in backward conditions (easily observable by a casual visitor), neither is permission to build or restore mosques forthcoming; Muslims have been particularly affected by expropriation of land for public use without adequate compensation, and the re-allocation of land in Western Thrace which began in 1967 has resulted in their receiving inferior land in exchange; Muslims are virtually excluded from the state bureaucracy and hindered in business matters by difficulties in obtaining business and driving licences and even subject to punitive levies; despite constitutional guarantees, Turks who leave Greece, even for a temporary period, have been denied re-entry under Article 19 of the Greek Nationality Law which states 'A person who is of foreign origin leaving Greek territories without the intention of returning may be deprived of Greek citizenship', and obtaining normal five-year passports is difficult for many Turks. This last point is illustrated by a number of cases, such as one reported in the Athens newspaper *Rizospastis* on 19 May 1986 that 'two Muslim origin Greek citizens' from a village near Komotini were refused re-entry and deported after having visited their son who was studying in Istanbul. Additionally it is alleged that the authorities are attempting to disperse the minority by moving unemployed Turks and Pomaks to other areas, where once registered they are unable to return to Western Thrace, and are pressured under pain of dismissal to change their names to Greek ones.

Education

In the vital field of education the Greek authorities have steadily increased teaching in Greek at the expense of Turkish. From the 1960s onwards religious teachers from the Arab world have progressively been reduced while the employment of teachers from Turkey to Turkish schools in Western Thrace has been stopped. Since 1968 only graduates from a special academy in Thessaloniki can be qualified to teach in Turkish schools. This academy takes much of its intake from Greek secondary schools and, its critics claim, relies on an outdated religious curriculum deliberately to create an incompetent hellenized education system in Western Thrace isolated from the mainstream of modern Turkish culture.

The situation has deteriorated with the authorities introducing an entrance exam for the two Turkish minority secondary schools in Komotini and Xanthi — there are some 300 Turkish primary schools — and a directorate from the government in March 1984 stipulating that graduate examinations from Turkish secondary and high schools have to be in Greek. The implementation of this law in 1985 with in some cases merely a few months' notice was extremely hard on the unfortunate students. The result of these measures has been a dramatic decline in secondary school students in Turkish schools from 227 in Xanthi and 305 in Komotini in 1983-4, to 85 and 42 respectively in 1986-7. Greek history books portray Turks in crude stereotypes and while Turkish pupils are allowed some books from Turkey there have been inexplicable delays resulting in long outdated textbooks having to be used.

The authorities have also prohibited the use of the adjective 'Turkish' in titles denoting associations etc. and the Turkish Teachers Association in Western Thrace was closed by order of Komotini court on 20 March 1986, a decision upheld by the Athens High Court on 28 July 1987.

Protest

As noted above, over a long period there have been many individual complaints by ethnic Turks at the deteriorating position of the minority in Western Thrace. Such protests are apparently gathering force. In the summer of 1988 there was a large-scale demonstration by Turks in Komotini which was followed by two bomb explosions — one in the central mosque and one in a cemetery of a neighbourhood mosque. Nobody was injured in these attacks which Turks see as an act of provocation by the Greeks against the Turkish minority. Additionally there have been a number of appeals by Turks in Western Thrace to outside bodies like the UN and Council of Europe. In August 1986 Sadik Ahmet, a doctor of philosophy from Western Thrace, was arrested along with a colleague and held for a few days. They were later tried in Thessaloniki and Sadik Ahmet was sentenced to two and a half years while his co-defendant received 15 months' imprisonment on charges of spreading false information and falsifying some five or six signatures after they had sent a petition containing some 13,000 signatures to the UN and the Council of Europe alleging a policy of assimilation and forced emigration by the Greek authorities and detailing many of the complaints listed above. Both were released pending appeal which was due to be held in December 1988 but has been postponed indefinitely apparently due to pressure by human rights groups like Amnesty International. On 18 June 1989 Sadik Ahmet stood for Parliament as an independent Turkish candidate and was elected with some 32% of the vote despite allegations of official pressure to disrupt his election campaign — illustrating the support for him among the Turkish population.

The situation appears to be becoming more serious with increased polarization of the communities in Western Thrace and while some of the complaints, like the alleged policy of resettling unemployed Turks in other areas being a deliberate policy of assimilation, may be exaggerated, the facts add up to an apparent deliberate policy of discrimination with a long term aim of assimilation akin to that carried out against the Macedonians by successive Greek governments. Against this escalating policy there appears to be growing discontent among the Turks in Western Thrace which might explode in the future.

The Gypsies and Albanians

The lack of statistics available for ethnic minorities and the official Greek position of classifying as Greeks all those who use Greek in everyday language — even if it is not their mother-tongue, especially if they are of Orthodox faith, again makes assessing the numbers of Gypsies, Albanians and Vlachs very hard. Estimates from official Greek sources give the figure for the **Gypsies** as far lower than outside observers who estimate the number at 140,000 of whom 45,000 are nomadic Muslims. Many Muslim Gypsies live in Macedonia and Western Thrace where there is a community of them, numbering 1500-2000, in Komotini alone. A previous MRG report[93] reported their plight, especially on the situation of Muslim Gypsies who lack citizenship and thus basic civil rights. A law passed in 1979 designed to enable them to obtain identity cards has had little apparent effect due to most of them lacking birth certificates. The Panhellenic Romani Association has held council elections in Thessaloniki and Athens since at least 1980 and about 50 houses have been built for Gypsies in Serrai. Muslim Gypsies have in practice only been accepted as Greek citizens after baptism and admission to the Orthodox Church, and the Bishop of Florina in Aegean Macedonia has continued to lead a church mission to convert Muslim Gypsies to Orthodoxy. The Ministry of Education is looking at the educational needs of the Muslim Gypsy population but travelling Gypsies are still faced with the 1976 law making camping illegal outside of organized sites — virtually all of which are for tourists and banned to Gypsies. The Gypsies, as is so common elsewhere, are at the bottom of the social order.

While there is much comment focused on the position of the Greek minority in Albania, there is very little information about the **Albanian** minority, a small number of whom lived in Western Aegean Macedonia, which remained in Greece after the founding of the Albanian state in 1913. Most of these Albanians were Orthodox by religion although there were Muslim Albanian Chams in northern Greece up till immediately after World War II. During the war attempts were made by the Italian occupiers to harness them against the Greeks and as a result there was a backlash against them with many being driven into Albania and mosques burnt. The Orthodox Albanians, similarly with other Orthodox minorities, tended to become Hellenicized due to the Greek control of the education system. Three generations ago there were many Albanian-speaking people in Attica, Boeotica, southern Euboea (Evvoia), and Hydra while the Plaka district in Athens by the Acropolis was the Albanian quarter of the city with its own law courts using the Albanian language.[94] However there is little sign of this minority today and it appears that the shared religion under Greek control and the education system has greatly facilitated their total and peaceful assimilation into the Greek nation.

The Vlachs (Koutsovlachs or Aromani)

The Vlachs are a latin-speaking people — they speak a form of Romanian — living south of Danube in Albania, Bulgaria, Yugoslavia (predominately in Serbia and Vardar Macedonia) and primarily in Greece. They are an historically old people who ante-date the more modern arrivals to the Balkan Peninsula like the Slavs, Bulgars and Turks. Perhaps because of this they, unlike other minorities, do not appear to live in particularly concentrated areas, with the exception of the 'Vlach capital' Aminciu (Metsovon) in the Pindus mountains at the headlands of the five rivers of the Pindus range. The censuses of 1935 and 1951 recorded 19,703 and 39,855 Vlachs respectively although as noted above the classification as Greek of those who use Greek as 'language of daily use' has tended to greatly underestimate the number of minorities like the Vlachs who tend to be hellenophile and are

almost entirely Orthodox Christians by religion (hence Greek Orthodox). Emigre Vlach sources claim a figure of 600,000 in Greece (although this would appear to be widely exaggerated).

In the area under study the Vlachs live in Aegean Macedonia, especially in villages in the mountainous regions, and are also present in Western Thrace. The area north-west of Polikastrion has a population of Meglen Vlachs who speak the Slav language as their mother tongue. The Vlachs are similar to the Sarakatsani — Greek-speaking transhumant shepherds — but less mobile and are seasonally nomadic as shepherds in the mountains while pursuing other fields of employment like medicine, law, taxi-driving etc.

Traditionally the Vlachs have held an important position in inland Greece and under the Ottoman domination they, due to their traditional occupations of shepherding and transport of goods by caravan, tended to control overland trade in the Greek provinces of the Ottoman empire while the Greeks controlled the sea trade. Many Vlachs identified themselves with Greeks due to having received Greek education in Greek schools, and took a leading role in the struggle for Greek independence. However some, influenced by the Romanian national movement and the close similarities between their languages, attempted to have church services and schooling in their vernacular — a move which, similarly to the Bulgarians (see above) was strongly resisted by the Greek Orthodox hierarchy. This latter strand of Vlach distinctness from Greeks was soon patronised by the new Romanian state leading to the creation of Romanian churches and schools in Macedonia, which was then still part of the Ottoman empire, funded by the Romanian state. In these schools children were taught the Vlach language, Aromanian, in the lower grades and then later Romanian, as it was a recognized literary language.[95] By 1912 the Romanian state was subsidizing over 30 such schools in Macedonia.

The savage internecine warfare in Macedonia from the 1890s to 1914 by rival armed bands of Serbs, Bulgarians and Greeks as the new national states competed for the decaying Ottoman empire was especially hard on the Vlachs who for the most part could not defend themselves well and there were massacres of Vlachs with churches and villages burnt by Greek nationalists. This sorry period finished after the settlement of the Balkan Wars and even in 1913 the Greek Prime Minister Venizelos signed an agreement with the Romanians to officially allow Romanian schools for Vlachs in the Greek state. The Vlach nationalist movement continued under Romanian tutelage but never recovered from the violence late in the 19th century.

The rise of fascism in Italy and Romania led to attempts, especially during the Italian occupation of parts of Greece during World War II, to harness the Vlachs to the fascist cause and an autonomous 'Principality of the Pindus' was even declared by an extremist named Alcibiades Diamandi of Samarina consisting of Epirus, Macedonia and all of Thessaly with Diamandi as Prince and a compatriot as head of the 'Roman Legion' — an army of Vlach fascists.[96] After World War II the new Romanian state chose not to carry on financing the schools and churches in Greece. In Macedonia during the Civil War, ELAS encouraged and defended the rights of Vlachs to use their language while the nationalist army brutally suppressed it.

The majority of activist Vlachs who saw themselves as distinct from Greeks tended to emigrate with the result that separatist feeling is much stronger in the diaspora than in the homeland — similarly with the Macedonians of Northern Greece. There is no apparent nationalist or separatist feeling among the Vlachs of Greece despite the occasional hostility towards them from the more nationalistic sections of Greek society usually manifested in objecting to the use of the Vlach language — it is frequently used in public places in Metsovon and elsewhere. An exaggerated example of this hostility is an article in the Athens newspaper *Stohos* — notorious for such outbursts against Greece's minorities — of 18 October 1984 which under the heading 'The end justifies the means' pointed to such public use of Vlach (and Macedonian) 'in the street, in the cafes and at work' and called for its prohibition by 'employing all means' against 'the plans of the enemies of the nation'. Such pressure has in the past tended to intimidate Vlachs living in the cities in mixed communities from speaking their own language and under the dictatorship of the Colonels from 1967 to 1974 Vlachs were even threatened with imprisonment for speaking Aromanian. However since the 1980s the situation has improved as the Greek government apparently recognizes that Vlachs unlike the Turks or Macedonians constitute no threat, real or potential, to the Greek state and many 'Vlach Cultural Societies' have come into existence. Since 1984 there has been a huge annual festival for all Vlach villages of Greece, and in the same year a newpaper for Vlachs *Avdhella* began publication in Greek. Despite this improvement the Greeks are still very wary of acknowledging any minorities and hold to the position that the Vlachs are Greeks who speak an unusual dialect. When Vlach activists in Germany contacted the European Community's Bureau of Lesser Known Languages which resulted in the European Community enquiring of Greece the position of the Vlachs there was a strong reaction within Greece involving leading Vlachs like Evangelos Averoff against this intervention from outside and a corresponding criticism of the burgeoning local cultural efforts. This has led to a severe limiting of previous efforts by Vlachs in Greece with only a few brave individuals speaking out against Averoff's view — such as Zoitsa Papazisi-Papatheodorou, a chemistry teacher from Trikala and a director of the Pan-Hellenic Vlach Cultural Society, who testified on behalf of the Vlach language to the European Community and as a result was vilified in the Greek press.

As noted above, large numbers of Vlachs emigrated during the course of the century and among these emigres there is some pro-Romanian feeling (due to lingustic and cultural similarities) and conversely some anti-Greek or anti-Yugoslav feeling. These emigres have formed Vlach associations in a number of places: France, USA, West Germany etc., and have held two international Vlach congresses in West Germany — in September 1985 in Mannheim, and in August 1988 in Freiburg. A central question at these conferences has been the lack of a defined Vlach language (there is however a Vlach-Romanian dictionary) and Vlachs from Greece pressed for the use of the Greek alphabet so as not to antagonize the Greek authorities; however the other participants preferred the more obvious choice of the Latin alphabet — the antagonism between 'Panhellenes' and 'Superromani', often becoming a struggle between Vlachs in Greece and those in the diaspora, is a constant factor in Vlach matters.

The Jews

Separate mention should be made concerning the fate of the Jews in the area under study. Large numbers of Spanish-speaking Sephardic Jews settled in the area after being expelled from Spain in the 16th century and, until World War II, Salonika (Thessaloniki or Solon — the main city in Macedonia) was predominately Jewish. The Jews were recognized as a separate *millet* by the Ottoman authorities and remained after the liberation of the area from Ottoman rule in the newly formed states of Bulgaria, Yugoslavia and Greece. The occupation of the area by Nazi Germany and her allies, Italy and Bulgaria, however saw the Jews once more faced by intolerance from the west, this time of a genocidal character.

In Bulgaria itself the situation was somewhat different to the other areas under study. Under Nazi pressure the Bulgarian government in October 1940 proposed several restrictions on the Jews but, in contrast to German laws, applied religious rather than racial criteria which allowed Jews to convert to Christianity to avoid persecution and the King delayed signing this obviously unpopular law until the end of January 1941 when Bulgaria's alliance with the axis powers was inevitable. Stiffer legislation including the wearing of the star of David was introduced in early 1942 and in August a Commissariat for Jewish Affairs (KEV) was set up in Sofia under Aleksander Belev which was to prepare to transfer Jews to the death camps in Poland. However massive opposition from prominent Bulgarians, including the King, deputies and leading church figures helped to save the Jews of Bulgaria from deportation and death and instead they were settled temporarily in the provinces and assembled in labour camps. As a result nearly all of Bulgaria's Jews, estimated at some 51,500, survived the war. However the period 1946-56 saw a mass exodus to Israel when almost 40,000 left Bulgaria and the population has dwindled to about 5000 and some observers say only 3000. The Sephardic Jews still remain a larger group than the Ashkenazim. They, along with the small number of Armenians, remain the only recognized minorities within Bulgaria today.[97]

The fate of the Jews in the occupied territories of Macedonia and Thrace was very different. Deportations began in March 1943 from Aegean and Vardar Macedonia and Greecian Thrace. The overwhelming majority perished in Treblinka concentration camp in Poland. The Jewish population of Greece, for example, was 63,200 in 1928, almost entirely Spanish speaking, according to official Greek statistics, but in 1951 the number was only 6325, while in the Socialist Republic of Macedonia the census of 1953 recorded only 55 Jews. In the Bulgarian occupied territories, responsibility for the transfer of the Jews to Nazi authority rested with KEV, and it appears that, despite Bulgarian claims to the contrary, the Jews in Macedonia and Thrace were knowingly transferred to their deaths by the Bulgarians — perhaps sacrificed for the sake of the Bulgarian Jews. The Nazi crime investigator, Simon Wiesenthal, confirmed on Skopje television in February 1986 that Aleksander Belev and Bulgarian ministers who signed documents on the liquidation of the Macedonian Jews in February and March 1943 were included in his list of war criminals.[98]

Albania

The Greeks

For centuries, Albania has suffered violent conquest at the hands of other countries. In 1912, when Albania freed itself from the Ottoman empire, it was the last country to achieve independence in the Balkans. It only retained this independence until 1939, when the Italian army invaded. The country won its freedom again in 1944. Hence, in modern history Albania has only been independent for a total of about 70 years. With this long tradition of foreign intervention, the current communist government which gained power in 1944 felt a clear need to forge an independent and unified nation. It perceived ethnic and religious diversity as a threat to this unity as well as evidence of prior foreign interventions. The Albanian government attacked diversity through a harsh anti-religion campaign and other measures.

The Greek minority in Albania is strongly rooted in a particular geographic region — the southernmost part of the country. The minority's identity also derives from its adherence to the (Greek) Orthodox Church and use of the Greek language and names. The Albanian government has attempted to eradicate all religious practice, Christian and Muslim; it has forbidden the use of 'foreign' and religious names; and it apparently discourages use of the Greek language in public places. It also reputedly moves non-Greeks into the Greek area and Greeks away from there — dispersing the Greek community. These policies affect non-Greek Albanians as well, but the Greek-Albanians constitute the largest and most identifiable minority and are thus particularly affected. By attacking diversity of any kind, the Albanian government is undercutting the fundamental sources of the Greek minority's identity.

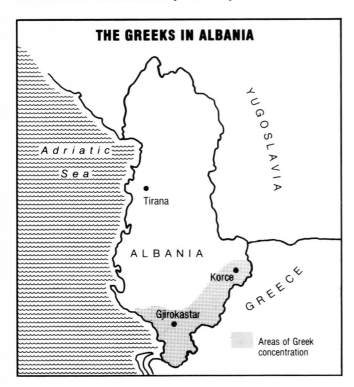

THE GREEKS IN ALBANIA

Adriatic Sea

YUGOSLAVIA

Tirana

ALBANIA

Korce

GREECE

Gjirokastar

Areas of Greek concentration

Albania may be viewed as comprised of three overlapping ethnic/religious communities; a small northern Catholic population; central and southern Orthodox and Greek Orthodox communities; and a generally dispersed Muslim population constituting some 70% of the population. Other small minorities exist in Albania, but they do not dominate any distinct geographic regions. According to the 1961 Albanian government census, 95% of the population is ethnically Albanian.[99] The remaining population is

comprised of 40,000 Greeks (2.4%), 15,000 Macedonians and Montenegrins (0.9%), 10,000 Vlachs (0.6%), and about 10,000 Gypsies.[100] Small Jewish and Armenian groups live in Albania as well.[101] Estimates of Albania's Greek minority range from 40,000 to 400,000. The lower figure is cited by the Albanian government. It may be limited to only those Greeks who reside in the two southern territories which the government formally acknowledges as being ethnically Greek. This figure would exclude Greeks living elsewhere. The maximum figure is also only an estimate since it is based on historical counts of Greeks in Albania, Greek schools and churches formerly in Albania, and individuals formerly registered with the Greek Orthodox Church of Albania.[102] Most analysts outside Albania place the number of Greeks somewhere between these two figures at about 200,000 to 250,000.[103]

Religion

The Albanian Constitution of 1976 is unique in that it expressly outlaws religion. Article 55 states, 'The creation of any type of organization of a fascist, anti-democratic, religious, or anti-socialist character is forbidden. Fascist, religious, warmongering, anti-socialist activity and propaganda are forbidden . . .' Article 55 of Albania's 1977 Criminal Code supports the Constitutional restrictions. 'Fascist, anti-democratic, religious, warmongering or anti-socialist propaganda, as well as the preparation, distribution, or the possession for distribution of literature with such a content in order to weaken or undermine the State of the dictatorship of the Proletariat are punishable by imprisonment of between three and ten years.'

These constitutional and legislative restrictions on religion serve to codify the Albanian government's continuing campaign against all religions. Previously more sporadic, the anti-religious campaign was formalized in 1967 during Albania's version of the Cultural Revolution. Decree No. 4236 in 1967 authorized local executive committees and cooperatives to expropriate all fixed assets and possessions of religious institutions without compensation. Religious buildings were closed or converted to other uses such as grain depots, theatres, coffee shops and stables. In September 1967, the government announced that it had closed all religious buildings, including 2169 churches, mosques, monasteries and other institutions.[104] Of these, 630 major Orthodox Churches were razed to the ground and an equal number were converted to other uses.[105]

Religious holidays and private religious practice were also suppressed. During the anti-religion campaign, authorities confiscated religious artifacts from individuals, including personal crucifixes, icons and bibles. Religious leaders were publicly denounced, shaven, defrocked, imprisoned and killed.[106] In April 1967, the 40 Greek Orthodox priests still alive were taken to the city of Delvino (some were taken out of prison for this purpose). There, in a public denunciation, they were shaven[107] and had their vestments removed and spat upon. One priest, Reverend Theodore Zisis, resisted the shaving and was consequently imprisoned for ten years.

The government has effectively eradicated formal religion in Albania, according to recent Greek minority escapees. Some individuals practise secretive and fragmentary religious observance in their homes, though even this religious practice risks punishment. One former resident of Albania said he knew of families that make Easter eggs, although they do so at night in their homes to avoid discovery and reprisals.[108] Another former resident said that he and his mother secretly wore crucifixes retained from before the anti-religion campaign; the crosses were sewn into their undergarments. He added that his mother hides an icon which she uses for prayer, but that people in his village are too afraid to observe religious rituals together. Former residents tell stories of people imprisoned for years or shot in the streets for possession of icons, bibles or crosses.

The anti-religious programme is effectively preventing young people from learning the religious practices and beliefs of their communities. Special civics classes teach schoolchildren to denounce family members and friends for religious observances and other activities. Some teachers force their students to break the fast of Lent by eating cheese. The suppression of religion is so complete that one former resident said he had never witnessed a religious practice until he was 18 years old, when he saw a woman bow over a candle in prayer.

The name-changing campaign

In 1975, the Albanian government mandated name-changes for 'citizens who have inappropriate names and offensive surnames from a political, ideological, and moral standpoint'.[109] Local civil affairs offices were supplied with lists of government-approved names. Although the Albanian government's name-changing programme has affected the whole country, it appears to have especially affected the Greek minority. According to one former resident, the Albanian government circulated a list of acceptable names to the Greek community as early as 1967-69. An Albanian scholar in the United States has written that the government 'issued the decree more for nationalistic than religious reasons, namely, to eliminate "alien influences" in the names of persons, as well as places, and replace them with what the regime regards as purely Albanian names.'[110] Another scholar stated, half in jest, 'There is no convincing evidence to suggest that the same policies were applied in the case of the Muslim majority. Had that been the case, [First Secretary] Hoxha [whose last name means Islamic priest in Albanian and Turkish] should have been the first one to change his own name, followed by four other Politburo members whose surnames are of religious origin.'[111] Recent escapees echo the observation of these scholars. Muslims have said that the name-changing campaign did not affect them, while virtually all Greek escapees could recount at least one instance of an imposed name-change.

The name-changing campaign disrupts longstanding traditions of the Greek community. Greeks name their children after their grandparents, or saints, martyrs or other religious figures.[112] Parents sometimes register an Albanian name with the government and use a Greek name with their child. Such children are reportedly forced to use their Albanian names in school.

Decree No. 225, also in 1975, concerned the changing of geographic place names with religious connotations. Towns named after Christian saints have been renamed.[113] Not only religious names have been changed, however; some non-religious Greek town names have been changed too.[114]

Administrative internment and other population movements

The Albanian government relocates individuals and families through an administrative process without formal adjudication. Laws relating to this procedure have been in existence for forty years; the current statute is Decree No. 5912 of 26 June 1979.[115] The decree specifies internment of those who 'represent a danger to the social system'. It also permits the internment of those persons whose relatives have fled Albania or gone into hiding inside the country.[116]

One former resident said that internment is usually for a five-year term, although this may be extended. Internees are sent from their region to work at agricultural cooperatives or factories in some other part of the country. Fenced-in camps served as places of internment. This practice may have changed recently. One former resident says that internees are now sent to remote villages and ordered to report daily to the local police. Those individuals who stray from the immediate area risk imprisonment. Several escapees state that they have heard that relatives have been sent into internment since they fled. One ethnic Greek escapee described his own internment experience and alleged that his family was not allowed to speak Greek and was forced to do the heaviest labour. Ethnic Greeks tend to be moved north away from their region and ethnic Albanians are moved south. After release, internees are reportedly allowed to return to their region of origin but not to their village; their homes are reputedly confiscated.

Permanent relocations are also occurring. Scholars are divided, however, as to the reasons for relocating families. Some say that the relocation is to disperse the Greek minority.[117] If a village is comprised of Greek minority residents, the village may obtain a Greek language school and other privileges. Minority status is granted only to wholly Greek villages; once two or three Albanian families arrive, the village loses that status.[118] Hence, the Albanian government may be using relocation to diminish the geographic scope of Greek minority legal rights. Other scholars say that relocations are purely for economic reasons and do not attack the Greek minority.[119]

Education

Greek language schools have existed in Albania since the 16th century. In 1922, the Albanian government reported to the League of Nations that 36 Greek schools existed in southern Albania.[120] Although the current number of schools is unknown, some do exist. There is one Greek language teacher-training college serving the community, and schools are provided with some Greek language texts, which on the evidence of those the authors have seen are in Greek with Albanian instructions. Interviews with former residents suggest, however, a significant decrease in the number of Greek schools in recent decades.[121] Also, Greek minority children attending Greek language schools are only taught in Greek during the first four years. Subsequently, students receive Greek instruction only as a foreign language or not at all.[122]

Restrictions on the use of the Greek language

Although there is no direct evidence of legal prohibitions against the use of Greek in public, many escapees have reported de facto restrictions in certain settings. A non-Greek escapee said that in his village none of the minorities there — Macedonian, Italian or Greek — were permitted to speak their own languages outside their homes. Some schools allegedly do not permit children to speak Greek to each other. It is also reported that Greeks in places of internal exile can only speak their language in their homes. One former resident has said that Greek may not be spoken during the compulsory military service. Amnesty International reports several complaints that Greeks are expressly forbidden to use Greek when visiting relatives in Albanian prisons.[123] There is however a weekly Greek language newspaper, some Greek publications and radio broadcasts in Greek.

Signs of change

First Secretary Enver Hoxha died in April 1985. His successor, First Secretary Ramiz Alia, may be easing the Albanian government's harsh policies. For example, visitors last year report extensive restoration of churches and mosques (as cultural relics and tourist sights).[124] More particularly with regard to the Greek minority, Albania has opened its border to allow Greek nationals to visit relatives in Albania and some Albanians to travel to Greece. Numbers have steadily increased: in 1948, 87 Albanians travelled to Greece; in 1985, that figure was 301; and in 1986, 535.[125] In 1985, 1265 Greeks travelled to Albania; the figure for 1987 was over 6000.[126] Cultural exchanges are also occurring between the two countries. The extent of these changes and their effect on human rights remains uncertain, however.

Yet the human rights record of the Albanian government is bleak. The Greek minority is at least recognized as such (in contrast to Turks in Bulgaria or Slav-Macedonians in Greece) although this does not prevent discrimination. While the government's policies have affected all sectors of the population, the Greek minority has been harshly affected. In its attempts to unify the country, the government undercuts fundamental bases of the Greek minority's identity. The abolition of religion has been disruptive to the Greek community whose cohesiveness depends on shared religious as well as ethnic ties. The mass of testimonies agree that the name-changing campaign focused on the non-Muslim sectors of the Albanian population. The government has attempted to eradicate the use of Orthodox and secular Greek names for people and places. Not all Greek children can attend schools where their own language is used for instruction or is even permitted among the students. Through internal exile and other population movements, the government is apparently weakening the Greek community. Areas designated as Greek may be losing their minority status — including the right to Greek-language schooling. Former residents report that the Greek language cannot be spoken in most public institutions and that most Greeks are afraid to speak their language outside their homes. Clearly, the Albanian government's attempts at forging a unified and uniform nation disregards the cultural rights of the Greek minority.

CONCLUSION

The problem of minorities in the area under study is acute. The most serious problems occur in Bulgaria where the authorities are using extreme coercive measures to forcibly assimilate its minorities, with the current exceptions of the small Jewish and Armenian populations. Where this has apparently failed in the case of the ethnic Turks, Bulgaria has resorted to forced migration. In Greece the authorities appear also to be pursuing a policy of creating a one-nation state by assimilation using education and economic pressure to achieve this. Although in Greece the level of pressure used is not comparable to that in Bulgaria the aim appears to be the same. Perhaps the high levels of state violence in Bulgaria is in part due to the shorter time-scale of the assimilations which while starting in the mid-1950s against the Macedonians (a special case for the Bulgarians) only really began in earnest in the early 1970s, while in Greece the assimilation of the Macedonians for example, has been in operation since Greece acquired the territories in 1913 after the Balkan wars and even earlier.

The time has come for states in the Balkans to reassess their own security, strategies and the prospects for social and economic development. The determination to create a homogeneous uni-ethnic nation state stemmed from the insecurity of new nation states and their consequent desire to establish a national identity. They were concerned that they should not be easily dismembered by external military adventurism (enemies might form an alliance with an internal ethnic group in the way that Hitler did in Czechoslovakia) and they believed that harmony could be established by removing diversity.

Yugoslavia, due to its inherent multi-nationalism and lack of a majority people, has opted for cultural diversity — in modern parlance the salad-bowl rather than the melting pot. However, within Macedonia, as elsewhere in Yugoslavia, the rise of Albanian nationalism has caused the authorities great alarm, compounded in Macedonia by official unease due to the relative infancy of the Macedonian nationhood, and they have reacted against the minority.

The growth of religious or national militancy poses major problems to governments throughout the world. Often they are symptoms of the denial of rights to minorities over many years, a feeling of exclusion from benefits of the state and a belief that as there is little to lose or that militant action offers the best chances of success. It is essential to tackle these root causes and not to heighten the feelings of injustice and exclusion through repression. Regrettably armies and police forces are rarely subtle in their approach, while politicians are rarely sufficiently self-confident and far-sighted to respond positively.

Throughout the Balkans religion has been and continues to be an important factor. Smaller Islamic minorities like the Pomaks have tended to become assimiliated by larger Islamic groups within the relevant countries — the Turks in Bulgaria and Greece, or, in Macedonia, the Albanians who have also tended to assimilate the Turks there resulting in the authorities in Macedonia encouraging these smaller Islamic groups to assert their separate identities. Minorities in all three countries who share the religion of the dominant group, Orthodoxy, have been or are being assimiliated, with far greater ease than the Muslims.

It remains to be seen how successful Bulgaria will be in its attempt to simultaneously deny the existence of, and forcibly assimilate such a large Islamic minority as its Turks — a minority with close ties through emigration and culture to a large neighbouring country. Up until May 1989 Bulgaria was able to keep the minority hermetically sealed from Turkey, apparently a precondition for success, but the changed international climate due to developments such as *Glasnost* in the USSR and elsewhere in Eastern Europe changed this and the current (at the time of writing in late September 1989) policy of forced migration is an illustration of the failure of this forced assimilation in the short term at least.

In Greece while the assimilation of the Macedonians, Vlachs and Albanians has apparently so far been successful it remains to be seen whether the Mulsim Turks of Western Thrace will be assimilated so easily. In Macedonia, and Yugoslavia in general, the nationality question is as alive as ever and when combined with the acute political and economic crisis gripping the country the future is unpredictable. Throughout the whole area the Gypsies remain at the bottom of the social scale although their very position has to an extent protected them from greater assimilation in the past. Developments beginning in Yugoslavia make the formation of greater self-awareness and corresponding political clout for the Gypsies a possibility — albeit only a distant future one.

Peaceful assimilation is to a large extent a natural process whereby an ethnic group, usually a small minority, over a period of time gradually coalesces from choice with another group, usually a dominant majority. At the other extreme is forcible assimilation whereby an ethnic group is usually denied the right to exist and its members are forced by pain of death or imprisonment to declare themselves to be part of another group and to abandon their customs and culture and adopt new ones. Between these two poles are a variety of others usually involving assimilation not so much by force as by control of the education system and the corresponding denial or restriction of educational rights to a particular minority. In the area under study almost every type of assimilation from the utilization of extreme force to that of apparent peace is being pursued.

It is clear today that the greatest threat to the security of many states is their internal conflicts with minorities and their failure to find strength in diversity. The repression of minorities has been shown to be an unsuccessful strategy fuelling conflicts and retarding development. MRG therefore urges all the governments in the region as a matter of urgency to review their practices towards minorities.

Footnotes

Footnotes have been kept to a minimum and where possible are incorporated into the text. Much of the information regarding the situation of the ethnic Turks in Bulgaria comes from over 100 interviews made, in the course of a number of trips to Turkey and Greece between January 1985 and June 1989, with recently arrived refugees from Bulgaria. Obtaining reliable figures for different ethnic groups in the area under study is hampered by the competing aspirations of the various nationalities/ethnic groups and their supporters abroad which has made statistics in the area, especially in Macedonia, notoriously suspect over a long period (see 'Maps and Politics' by H.R. Wilkinson).

RFE = Radio Free Europe

BTA = Bulgarian Telegraph Association

[1] Statisticheski Godishnik na Narodna Republika Bulgaria 1985 (all census figures unless indicated are official ones).

[2] Predrag Vukovic, 'U Sluzbi Starog', Politika, Belgrade, 7 December 1975.

[3] Bulgaria: Imprisonment of Ethnic Turks, Amnesty International EUR/15/03/86, p 26.

[4] R. King — Minorities under Communism, Nationalities as a source of tension among Balkan Communist States, Cambridge, Mass, Harvard University Press 1973, pp 188/9.

[5] Amnesty International, op.cit., p 26.

[6] NIN, Belgrade, 5 January 1975.

[7] RFE Research Bulgaria SR/2, 12 March 1985, p 5.

[8] Amnesty International, op.cit., p 27.

[9] Ibid.

[10] Huseyin Memisoglu, Bulgarian Oppression in Historical Perspective, Ankara, 1989, p 26.

[11] Amnesty International, op.cit., p 28.

[12] Ibid.

[13] Memisoglu, op.cit., p 26.

[14] European Parliament Working Document 2-1199/85.

[15] Amnesty International, op.cit., pp 3-4 and Bihal Simsir — The Turks of Bulgaria, London, 1988, pp 245-264.

[16] Reported by Tanjug on 28 March 1985 in BBC SWB EE/7914/B/1, April 1985.

[17] Rabotnichesko Delo, Sofia, 19 April 1971.

[18] From paper by Wolfgang Hoepken, Institute of S.E. European Studies, Munich, for Refugee Studies Programme, Oxford University, 8 February 1988.

[19] Ibid.

[20] Dragoljub K. Budimovski — Makedontsite vo Albanija, NIP 'Studenski Zbor', Skopje, 1983.

[21] Amnesty International, op.cit., p 6.

[22] Op.cit. as note 16.

[23] Amnesty International, op.cit., p 16.

[24] RFE Bulgaria SR, 8 April 1988.

[25] Amnesty International, op.cit., p 17.

[26] BTA, Sofia, 5 April 1988.

[27] Bulgaria: Continuing Human Rights Abuses against Ethnic Turks — Amnesty International, EUR/15/01/87, p 5.

[28] Op.cit. as note 16.

[29] Otkrito Pismo na Grupa Balgari ot Narodna Republika Balgaria Vazstanovili Svoite Balgarski Imena — Sofia Press, 1985.

[30] See statement by Valentin Bojilov, Deputy Permanent Representative of P.R. Bulgaria to UN in Geneva, at the Sub-Commission on the Prevention of Discrimination and Protection of Minorities, 38th Session, 26 August 1985.

[31] Stefan Troebst — Stories from the Politburo and 1001 Nights: the Aggravation of the Bulgarian Assimilation Politics against the Turkish Minority.

[32] Tanjug, 8 January 1986, in BBC SWB EE/8153/B3, 10 January 1986.

[33] Memorandum and Press Release, March 1985 from the Bulgarian Press Office in London.

[34] Amnesty International, Imprisonment of Ethnic Turks, p 13.

[35] Ibid., p 20.

[36] Deputy Foreign Minister Ivan Ganev at Sofia Press Conference reported in the Guardian Weekly, 2 July 1985.

[37] Reuter, 18 May 1989.

[38] Turgut Ozal reported in BBC World Service, 18 June 1989.

[39] RFE Weekly Record of Events in Eastern Europe, Bulgaria, 1 to 7 June 1989.

[40] The Independent, London, 24 June 1989.

[41] BBC World Service, 23 June 1989, and Guardian Weekly, 2 July 1988.

[42] Ozal, op.cit. as note 38.

[43] RFE Weekly Record of Events in Eastern Europe, Bulgaria, 18 to 24 May 1989.

[44] Amnesty International, UA 173/89 EUR 15/04/89, 9 June 1989.

[45] Amnesty International, 'Bulgaria: Imprisonment of Ethnic Turks and Human Rights Activists', EUR 15/01/89.

[46] RFE Weekly Record of Events in Eastern Europe, Bulgaria, 8 to 14 June 1989.

[47] The Independent, as note 40.

[48] E. Barker — Macedonia: its Place in Power Politics, (Register of research in the Social Sciences in progress and in plain No.7, 1949-1950) Cambridge, London, 1950.

[49] The most comprehensive refutation is 'Edinstvoto na Balgarskiya Ezik b Minaloto i Dnes', published by the Bulgarian Academy of Sciences, Sofia, 1978.

[50] E.g. Istorija za VII Oddelenie, (IV Izdanie), Skopje, 1980.

[51] Yugoslavia: Prisoners of Conscience — Amnesty International, EUR/48/20/85, pp 41-2.

[52] Figures from 'Much Discomfort in Macedonia' — Viktor Meier, Frankfurter Allgemeine, 23 June 1983, p 10.

[53] From 'Schools and Education' — Risto Kantardzhiev and Lazo Lazaroski in The Socialist Republic of Macedonia — edited by Mihailo Apostolski and Haralampie Polenkovich, p 110.

[54] Amnesty International, op.cit., p 12.

[55] Yugoslavia: Recent Events in the Autonomous Province of Kosovo, Amnesty International, Eur 48/08/89.

[56] Tanjug, 7 May 1984, in BBC SWB EE/7639/B/9, 10 May 1984.

[57] Belgrade Home Service, 23 February 1988, in BBC SWB EE/0084/B/5, 25 February 1988.

[58] Amnesty International, op.cit.

[59] Djordje Jankovic in Vjesnik, Zagreb, 12 October 1986, p 7.

[60] IRNA (Iranian report), 13 December 1986, in BBC SWB EE/8444/B/19, 17 December 1986.

[61] Ilija Josifovski — Opshtestvenite Promeni na Selo: Makedonskoto, Albanskoto i Turskoto Naselenie na Selo vo Polog: Sotsioloshka Studija, published by the Institute of Sociological, Political and Juridicial Research, Skopje, 1974.

[62] Paul Shoup — Communism and the Yugoslav National Question, New York 1968, pp 181/2, and Stephen Palmer and R. King — Yugoslav Communism and the Macedonian Question, Hamden, Connecticut, Archon Books, 1971, p 178.

[63] Duga — Belgrade, 8 May 1982, pp 18/9.

[64] Tanjug, 21 September 1987, in BBC SWB EE/8683/B/7, 26 September 1987.

[65] Op.cit. as note 63.

[66] Op.cit. as note 53.

[67] Oslobodjenje — Sarajevo, 6 January 1989.

[68] Op.cit. as note 63.

[69] See Roma: Europe's Gypsies — MRG Report No.14, Gratton Puxton, pp 11/12.

70 For a recap of Dr. Trifunoski's findings in Ovce Polje and other references see 'Tzintzari in Ovce Polje in S.R. Macedonia' by Dragoslav Antonijevic — *Balkanica V*, Belgrade, 1975.

71 Todor Simovski — 'The Balkan Wars and their Repercussions on the Ethnical Situation in Aegean Macedonia', *Glasnik* Vol.XVI, No.3, Skopje, 1972, (printed in *op.cit.* as note 53, p 191).

72 'Macedonian National Minorities in Greece, Bulgaria and Albania' by Hristo Andonovski, p 192, in *The Socialist Republic of Macedonia*, edited by Mihailo Apostoloski and Harampie Polenakovich, Skopje 1974, and *op.cit.* as note 48.

73 Tosho Popovski — *Makedonskoto Natsionalno Maltsinstvo vo Bulgarija, Grtsija i Albanija*, Skope, 1981, p 72.

74 *Op.cit.* as note 72, pp 198/9.

75 *Istoriyata na Makedonskiot Narod, Kniga III*, published by NIP Nova Makedonija, Skopje, 1969, pp 271/5.

76 *Ibid.*, p. 274.

77 Hans-Joachim Hoppe, 'Bulgarian Nationalities Policies in Occupied Thrace and Aegean Macedonia', in *Nationalities Papers*, Spring-Fall 1986, Vol. XIV, No.1-2, pp 89-100.

78 According to Greek newspaper *Elefteron Vima*, 19 October 1952, referred to in *op.cit.* as note 73, p 76.

79 Lazo Mojsov — *Okoly Prashanjeto na Makedonskoto Natsionalno Maltsinstvo vo Grtsija*, published by the Institute for National History, Skopje, 1954, p 17.

80 *Op.cit.* as note 73, p 223.

81 *Op.cit.* as note 72, p 196.

82 Richard Clogg, *A Short History of Modern Greece*, Cambridge University Press, 1979, p 164.

83 *Op.cit.* as note 72, p 196.

84 Tanjug, 6 June 1988, in BBC SWB EE/0172/A1/3, 8 June 1988.

85 Reuter 201651 GMT of 30 June 1988.

86 Tanjug, 15 May 1986, in BBC SWB EE/8262/A1/6, 19 March 1986.

87 *Ibid.*

88 Tanjug, 19 April 1986, in BBC SWB EE/8238/A1/1, 21 April 1986.

89 *Vecernje Novosti*, 10 June 1988, in BBC SWB EE/0177/i, 14 June 1988.

90 F. De Jong — *Names, Religious denomination and Ethnicity in Western Thrace*, Leiden/E.J. Brill/1980.

91 Clogg, *op.cit.*, p 215.

92 For this and following section see F. De Jong — 'Muslim Minorities in Western Thrace', in *World Minorities in the Eighties*, edited by Georgina Ashworth, Quartermaine House Ltd. and MRG 1980.

93 MRG No.14, *op.cit.*, p 8.

94 J.G. Nandris — The Thracian Inheritance, *The Illustrated London News*, June 1980, p 10.

95 See a series of Articles in *The Greek American* by N. Balamaci — 'One View from the Diaspora', 12, 19, 26 September and 3 October 1987; 26 August, 2 ,9, 16 September 1989.

96 See *The Call of the Earth* by Evangelos Averoff-Tossizza, Caratzas Brothers, New Rochelle NY, 1981 and review of the above by N. Balamaci in *The Newsletter of the Society Farsarotul*, Vol. II, issue 2 of August 1988, pp 19-22.

97 See *op.cit.* as note 77 for Bulgaria's treatment of the Jews in World War II.

98 Tanjug, 20 February 1986, in BBC SWB EE/8190/A1/2, 22 February 1986.

99 P. Prifti, *Socialist Albania since 1944: domestic and foreign developments* (1978). In 1976, the country's population was approximately 2,500,000.

100 *Ibid.* citing R. Marmullaku, *Albania and the Albanians* (1975).

101 Kamm, 'An Albanian Jew Flees, With Grim Tale to Tell', *New York Times*, 30 August 1986.

102 Interview with Konstantinos Gigas of the Committee for the Struggle of Northern Epirus, Athens, March 1988.

103 For example, one writer states that 250,000 is more realistic. Stavrou, 'Inside Albania's brutal system of political prisons', *Minneapolis Star & Tribune*, 4 February 1985. Greek Minister of State for Foreign Affairs, Karolos Papoulias, once cited a figure of 200,000 for the Greek minority in Albania. Modiano, 'Greeks in Albania allowed closer links with Athens', *New York Times*, 21 December 1984.

104 Amnesty International, *Albania: Political imprisonment and the law*, 13 (1984).

105 *Human Rights in Albania: Hearing Before the Sub-committee on Human Rights and International Organizations of the House Comm. on Foreign Affairs*, 98th Cong., 2nd Sess. 14, 25 January 1984, (statement of Nikolaos A. Stavrou, Ph.D., Professor of Political Science, Howard University).

106 *Ibid.*, p 13.

107 Since beards are associated with Orthodox priests, the wearing of beards was outlawed. Until 1983, foreign visitors were shaved at customs.

108 Interview with a former resident of Albania who recently escaped. Since it was impossible for the authors (MLIHRC) to send an investigating mission to Albania it has concentrated on interviewing former Albanian residents who recently escaped from that country. It has also collected a great deal of written documentary evidence and has attempted to cross-check and corroborate allegations made by former residents. In order to protect these informants they are not referred to by name.

109 Administrative Decree 5339, cited in PRIFTI, *op.cit.* as note 99, p 164.

110 *ibid.*

111 Stavrou, *Albania: The Politics of Religious Persecution in Albania*, presented at the RCDA conference 'The Balkans and the Soviet Union: Religious Freedom, Human Rights and International Relations' at Marymount College, Arlington, VA, 21-23 May 1986.

112 Stavrou statement, as note 105.

113 E.G. Agios Nikolaos ('St. Nicholas'), an ethnically Greek village had its name changed to Drita ('Light').

114 Stavrou statement, *op.cit.* as note 105, e.g. Mavropoulo ('Black City' in Greek) became Buronjq ('Shield' in Albanian.

115 Amnesty International, *op.cit.*, pp 26-7.

116 *Ibid.*

117 International Federation for the Protection of the Rights of Ethnic, Religious, Linguistic and other Minorities, IFPRERLM, *The State of Religious and Human Rights in Albania: Preliminary Report at 15 (no date given)*.

118 Interview with former resident. See also IFPRERLM, *The State of Religious and Human Rights in Albania*, submitted at the 39th Session of the United Nations Sub-Commission on Prevention of Discrimination and Protection of Minorities, Geneva, pp 3-5 (1987).

119 'Movements from South to North and vice-versa . . . are part of an incessant transfer of labour reserves in the industrialization process of the country'. *Human Rights in Albania: Hearing Before the Sub-Comm. on Human Rights and International Organizations of the House Comm. on Foreign Affairs*, 98th Cong., 2nd Sess., 25 January 1984 (testimony by Sami Repishti) reprinted in part in *V Albanian Catholic Bulletin* 63, 64 (Nos.1 and 2, 1984).

120 *Report from the Albanian Minister for Foreign Affairs*, Tirana, Albania, 7 July 1922, reprinted in *Minority Schools in Albania* (Alb.), 1935 P.C.I.J., ser. C, No. 76, Pleadings pp 40, 42.

121 One former resident cites two school closings in particular. Also refer to text above at footnotes 117 and 118.

122 Stavrou statement, *op.cit.* as note 105, p 16.

123 Amnesty International, *op.cit.*.

124 Interviews in June 1989 with the Imam Vehbi Ismail of the Albanian Islamic Center, Harper Woods, Michigan; and the Very Reverend Arthur Liolin, Chancellor of the Albanian Orthodox Archdiocese, Boston, Massachusetts.

125 Interview with Helena Smith, Associated Press, Athens, March 1989.

126 Cowell, 'A Hint of Change in the Albanian Air', *New York Times*, 20 June 1988.

Very Select Bibliography

BARKER, Elizabeth, *Macedonia: Its Place in Balkan Power Politics*, London, 1950.

CLOGG, Richard, *A Short History of Modern Greece*, Cambridge University Press, 1979.

CRAMPTON, R.J., *A Short History of Modern Bulgaria*, Cambridge University Press, 1987.

JELAVICH, Barbara and Charles, *Nationalism in the Balkans 1804-1920*, University of Washington Press, Seattle/London.

LENDVAI, Paul, *Eagles in Cobwebs; Nationalism and Communism in the Balkans*, Doubleday, New York, 1969.

PALMER, Stephen and KING, Robert, *Yugoslav Communism and the Macedonian Question*, Hamden, Connec, Archon Books, 1971.

PRIFTI, Peter, *Socialist Albania since 1944: Domestic and Foreign Developments*, MIT, Cambridge, Mass./London, 1978.

PUXTON, Gratton, *Roma: Europe's Gypsies*, MRG Report No.14.

SHOUP, Paul, *Communism and the Yugoslav National Question*, New York, 1968.

STAVRIANOS, L.S., *The Balkans since 1453*, New York, 1958.

SUGAR, P., *South Eastern Europe under Ottoman Rule 1354-1804*, University of Washington Press, Seattle/London.

SWIRE, J., *Bulgarian Conspiracy*, London, 1939.

WACE, A.J.B. and THOMPSON, M.S., *Nomads of the Balkans*, Methuen, 1914.

WILKINSON, H.R., *Maps and Politics, A Review of the Ethnographic Cartography of Macedonia*, Liverpool, 1951.

WINNIFRITH, Tom, *The Vlachs*, Duckworth, 1987.

The things they say about us ...

" **Great accuracy and detail** "

The Times

" **Systematically documented and unemotionally analysed** "

The Internationalist

" **Excellent** "

Peace News

" **Fair and unbiased** "

The Times

" **The best analysis** "

The Economist

" **A fascinating study** "

New Society

" **Timely and objective** "

The Times

" **Valuable insight** "

The Friend

FOR JUST £12 (UK) OR £14 / US $25 (OVERSEAS) MRG will send you the next FIVE minority reports:

You will receive, post free, new reports automatically — and at a significantly lower price.

In addition, you will be helping MRG, enabling us to commission more reports from the ever-growing number of situations which need investigation — refugees, migrant workers, the oppression of women, threatened indigenous peoples, destructive ethnic and religious conflicts, and many others.

SUBSCRIPTIONS
cost only £12 (UK) or
£14/US$25 (overseas)
and entitle you to the next five
MRG reports, post free.

FREE SUBSCRIPTION
Order a full set of reports at the discounted price and receive a free subscription. Our full range of over 80 reports, plus the subscription, costs only £125 (UK) or £175/US$275 (overseas) — postage included — a saving of up to 20%.

SEND FOR FULL DETAILS NOW:

THE MINORITY RIGHTS GROUP
29 CRAVEN STREET
LONDON WC2N 5NT

DR 24 .P6 1989

Poulton, Hugh.

Minorities in the Balkans

DATE DUE

OCT 18 '90			

HIGHSMITH   # 45220

GENERAL THEOLOGICAL SEMINARY
NEW YORK